Michelle Worg

Move!

Preparation for the A1 Movers Cambridge English Qualifications

Student's Book

The pleasure of learning

PUBLISHING

Contents

Hello!

1 🔊**1 Say hello! Look and listen. Then complete.**

Hello! I'm Lucy. I'm _____.

Hi! My name's Tom. I'm _____.

Who's that?

Zoe!

11 . 12 . 13 . 14 . 15 . 16 . 17 . 18 . 19

2 Read and match.

1 What's your name?

2 How old are you?

3 Who's that?

4 How do you spell it?

a Z-O-E.

b I'm ten.

c Nick.

d It's Zoe.

3 Look at the picture. Find and say the numbers 20 to 100.

4 **Write the numbers.**

twenty-seven _____   ninety-nine _____

forty-one _____   seventy-five _____

eighty-three _____   thirty-six _____

sixty-four _____   fifty-eight _____

5 **Look and complete.**

first • second • third • fourth • fifth

Ann's picture is in <u>first</u> place.
1 Lucy's picture is in _____ place.
2 Tom's picture is in _____ place.
3 Matt's picture is in _____ place.
4 Grace's picture is in _____ place.

6 **Say & Play Play a game.**

1 My family

1 🔊2 **Listen to Lucy. Look and point.**

2 🔊3 **Look and complete. Listen and check.**

aunt • brother • cousin (x 2) • father • ~~grandfather~~
grandmother • sister • uncle • mother

Peter
grandfather

Mary
_____

Lily
_____

Fred
_____

Dan
_____

Jane
_____

Vicky
_____

Lucy
ME!

Charlie
_____

Jack
_____

Clare
_____

3 🔊 4 **Read and complete. Listen and check.**

> granddaughters • son • grown-ups • parents • daughter
> grandparents • grandson • grandchildren

Lily and Fred are Lucy's <u>parents</u>.
1 Jack is Jane's _____.
2 Clare is Dan's _____.
3 Vicky, Lucy and Clare are Mary and Peter's _____.
4 Mary and Peter are Lucy's _____.

5 Charlie is Mary and Peter's _____.
6 Lucy and Charlie are Peter's _____.
7 Peter, Mary, Lily, Fred, Jane and Dan are all _____.

4 🔊 5 **Circle the correct word. Listen and check.**

Peter has got **a beard /** (**glasses**) and grey hair.
1 Fred is **thin / fat** and has got **glasses / a moustache**.
2 Dan is **short / tall** and has got **fair / black** hair.
3 Jane has got **curly / straight** brown hair.
4 Vicky has got **curly / straight** black hair.

Look & Learn

Order of adjectives

long curly fair hair

5 🔊 6 **Listen and choose.**

1 A ☐   B ☐   C ☐

2 A ☐   B ☐   C ☐

3 A ☐   B ☐   C ☐

4 A ☐   B ☐   C ☐

6 Say & Play **Student A, describe a person from Lucy's family but make one mistake. Student B, find the mistake!**

> Mary has got long brown hair.

> No, Mary hasn't got... She's got...

7 🔊7 **Listen and read.**

> This is Nick. He's very tall and thin.

> And this is my friend, Eva. She's got beautiful black hair.

> These two boys are Alex and Sam. They're brothers.

> Is this girl in your class, too?

> No, Dad. That's Miss Day! She's young and she's my teacher!

Look & Learn

He's very tall. ---> 's = **is**

She's got black hair. ---> 's = **has**

▶ *be* and *have got* p. 139

8 **Read and complete.**

Daisy _is_ tall. She _hasn't got_ red hair.

1

My brother and sister _____ black hair.

2

My cousin _____ thin.

3

Ann is short. She _____ long fair hair.

4

My grandparents _____ grey hair.

5

My uncle _____ a beard.

9 Read and complete.

Hi! I'm Matt. Let me tell you about my family.

This is my Aunt Sally. She's short and thin.

She (1) _____ black hair, she's got short fair hair.

My uncle is called Ben. Uncle Ben (2) _____ curly brown

hair. He's also got a (3) _____ and a beard.

My grandfather Hugo is (4) _____ because he eats a lot!

My grandmother Grace (5) _____ fat because she loves

doing sport. Both my grandparents (6) _____ grey hair.

My sister's name is Alice. She (7) _____ very tall.

My sister and I have both got (8) _____ hair and green

eyes. I love my family. We are all different!

10 Say & Play Look at the cards and play the game.

She's tall and thin.

Has she got glasses?

No, she hasn't.

Is it Sue Green?

Yes, it is!

Listening Part 5

1 🔊8 **Listen and colour and write. There is one example.**

Listen for the words *colour* or *write*. When you hear the colour, draw a short line with your crayon inside the object. You can finish colouring it later.

Speaking Part 1

2 🔊9 **Listen and find the differences.**

Describe the differences in the two pictures using *Here..., but here...*

3 ▶ **Now watch the video and talk about your answers.**

2 My week

1 🔊10 **Listen to Tom. Look and point.**

A [____]

B Monday

C [____]

D [____]

E [____]

F [____]

G [____]

2 🔊10 **Listen again and write the words.**

Monday • Tuesday • Wednesday
Thursday • Friday • Saturday • Sunday

Look & Learn

Don't forget to start days of the week with a **capital letter**!

3 🔊11 **Say the Sounds Say the chant.**

Monday, Tuesday, Wednesday
What's your favourite day?
Thursday, Friday, Saturday, Sunday
My favourite day is today!

4 **Look at the pictures on page 12 again. Complete Tom's week.**

ride my bike • learn the guitar • draw pictures • watch TV • h̶a̶v̶e̶ ̶m̶y̶ ̶E̶n̶g̶l̶i̶s̶h̶ ̶l̶e̶s̶s̶o̶n̶
take photos • go to Lucy's house • go swimming

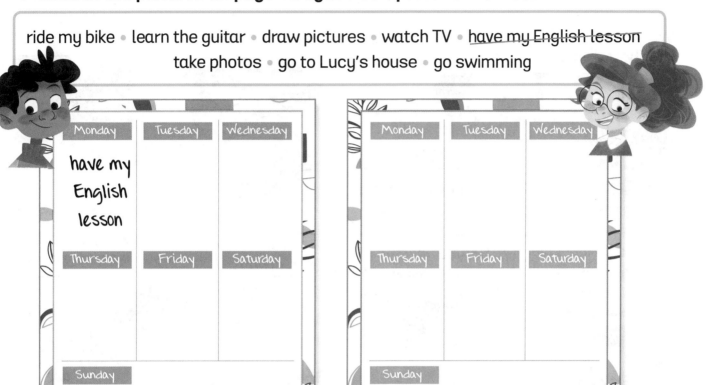

Monday	Tuesday	Wednesday
have my English lesson		
Thursday	Friday	Saturday
Sunday		

Monday	Tuesday	Wednesday
Thursday	Friday	Saturday
Sunday		

5 **Read about Lucy's week and write about it above.**

My Week

On Monday mornings, I have my English lesson with Tom.
We sometimes go to the library. I like those days best! In the afternoon,
I have a piano lesson. On Tuesday afternoons, I play football with my friends.
On Wednesdays, I ride my bike. Tom comes to my house on Thursdays and we
play games with my brother, Charlie. On Fridays, I go with Charlie to basketball
practice. At the weekend I don't do much sport. I listen to music and sing my
favourite songs on Saturdays. And on Sundays I do my homework!

6 **Work in pairs. Find four differences between Tom and Lucy's week.**

On Tuesdays, Lucy plays football. Tom has got a guitar lesson.

7 **What do you do every week?**
Tell your partner.

On Mondays, I do my homework.
At the weekend...

Look & Learn

I do my homework **on Mondays**.
I ride my bike **at the weekend**.

My week

8 🔊12 **Listen and read.**

> Wow! 10/10 in English! That's fantastic!

> Thanks, Lucy. Miss Day is a great teacher!

> Yes, she is. But I don't always understand everything. I sometimes make mistakes.

> Hmm, do you always listen in class?

> Yes, I do! And I do my homework.

> Do you *always* do your homework?

> Well... not always.

> Come on, we can do our homework now!

9 **Look and complete.** ▶ Present simple p. 140

| Monday | Tuesday | Wednesday | Thursday | Friday | Saturday | Sunday |

1 Zoe _____ TV on Fridays.

2 Zoe _____ pictures on Wednesdays.

3 Zoe _____ a bike on Mondays. She _____ a bike on Thursdays.

4 Zoe _____ computer games on Saturdays. She _____ computer games on Sundays.

10 **Look at the pictures in exercise 9 again. Ask and answer questions.**

When does Zoe ride a bike?

On Thursdays. Does she play computer games on Saturdays?

Yes, she does. / No, she doesn't.

11 **Write the adverbs.**

sometimes • always / every day • never • often

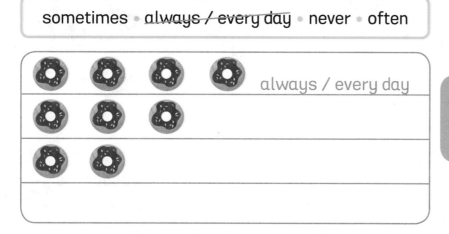

always / every day

Look & Learn

I'm **always** at home after dinner.
I **often** ask questions.
We don't speak English **every day**.

12 **Put the words in order.**

on Thursdays. / go to / I / the park / sometimes
I sometimes go to the park on Thursdays.

1 My / brother / draws / never / pictures.
2 go to / the countryside / We / often / on / Sundays.
3 don't / on / Saturdays. / always / I / see / my grandmother
4 teacher / homework / My / every day. / doesn't / give us
5 after school. / sometimes / friends / play / My / computer games

13 **Say & Play** **Choose three cards then make sentences and questions.**

Reading and Writing Part 2

1 Read the text and choose the best answer.

Example

Jim   Hi Sally. What are you doing?

Sally   **A** Yes, I am.

       B I watch TV on Fridays.

       C I'm doing my homework.

> Read the question. Think about the answer. Then read options A-C. Look for words like *do*, *is / are* and *can*.

Questions

1 Jim   I'm going to the park later. Do you want to come?

    Sally   **A** Yes, please!

         B Yes, I am.

         C No, I haven't.

2 Jim   We can ride our bikes there. Have you got a bike?

    Sally   **A** No, but I can take my skateboard.

         B Yes, I can.

         C My bike is red.

3 Jim   Do you often go to the park?

    Sally   **A** I don't like it.

         B I sometimes go at the weekend.

         C No, thank you.

4 Jim   Do you like seeing the ducks on the lake?

    Sally   **A** It's funny!

         B They're swimming.

         C Yes, I love them!

5 Jim   Let's take some bread for the ducks.

    Sally   **A** That's a great idea!

         B They're hungry.

         C Yes, that's right.

6 Jim   Oh, no! It's raining!

    Sally   **A** OK, it's bad.

         B Let's go tomorrow.

         C We never go there.

Speaking Part 3

2 🔊13 **Listen and say which one is different.**

Speaking Part 4

3 **Complete the questions. Then ask and answer questions with your partner.**

Listen to the questions. When the question uses *Why*, use *because* to answer.

Student A

1 What activities _____ (you / do) in your free time?
2 _____ (you / like) playing sports?
Which sports _____ (you / play)?
3 When _____ (you / go) to the park?

Student B

1 What activities _____ (you / do) at school?
2 _____ (you / like) watching TV or reading books? Why?
3 _____ (you / have) any classes after school?
When _____ (you / go) to these classes?

4 ▶ **Now watch the video and talk about your answers.**

17

1 🔊14 **Listen. Look and point.**

2 🔊15 **Write the numbers. Listen and check.**

address	8	downstairs	☐	
balcony	☐	shower	☐	
toothpaste	☐	toothbrush	☐	
basement	☐	upstairs	☐	
lift	☐	towel	☐	

lift (UK)
elevator (US)

3 🔊16 **Say the Sounds Listen and say this three times.**

Where's my **to**wel?
I'm **dow**nstairs in the **sho**wer.
I need my **to**wel now!

4 Write the words.

> ~~stairs~~ • bookcase • balcony • mirror • lift • armchair • bath • bed
> cupboard • desk • towel • lamp • basement • sofa
> computer • toothpaste • rug • toothbrush • roof

Bathroom	Bedroom	Living room	Apartment building
_____	_____	_____	stairs, _____
_____	_____	_____	_____
_____	_____	_____	_____

5 🔊17 Listen and look at the picture on page 18 again. Then match and say.

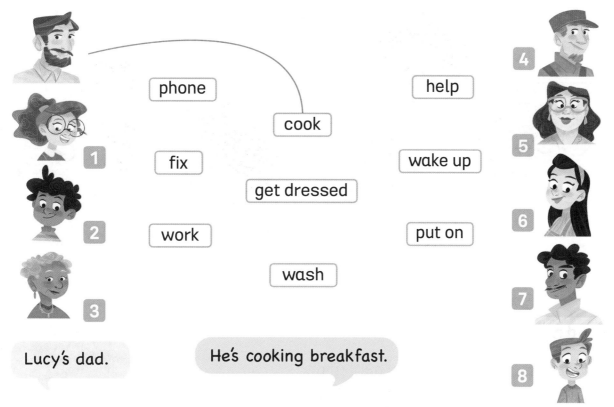

phone

cook

help

fix

wake up

get dressed

work

put on

wash

Lucy's dad.

He's cooking breakfast.

6 Say & Play Look at the pictures. Find five funny mistakes.

He's going to school with no shoes on!

He's...

3 At home

7 🔊18 **Listen and read.**

Can you answer the phone, Lucy? I'm washing my hands.

Hi Lucy! What are you doing?

Hi! I'm cooking with Vicky. Sorry, Tom. I'm busy.

This isn't a very good birthday! I'm not having fun.

What a surprise for Tom!

In the afternoon...

Surprise!

Happy birthday, Tom!

▶ Present continuous p. 140

8 **Read and complete.**

Vicky ___is washing___ (wash) her hands.

1 Zoe _____ (put on) a hat.
2 Lucy _____ (talk) on the phone.
3 Vicky and Lucy _____ (make) a cake.
4 They _____ (not cook) dinner.
5 Tom _____ (not enjoy) himself.
6 Now Tom _____ (smile) again.

Look & Learn

He is ---▶ He's
They are ---▶ They're

9 **Ask and answer questions.**

Is Vicky washing her hands?

Yes, she is.

10 Look and correct the sentences.

1 The young man is taking off his coat.

He isn't taking off his coat.

He's putting on his hat.

2 The boy is having a shower.

3 The woman is going to bed.

4 The man is having dinner.

5 The children are watching TV.

6 The woman is fixing the television.

7 The girls are taking the lift upstairs.

11 Write questions and answers.

1 What / young man / put on?

A What is the young man putting on?

B He's putting on his hat.

2 Why / boy / wash his face?

A _____

B _____

3 When / woman / work?

A _____

B _____

4 Who / cook / dinner?

A _____

B _____

5 What / children / do?

A _____

B _____

6 Where / woman / fix the car?

A _____

B _____

12 Say & Play Look at the cards then ask and answer. Tick (✔) or cross (✗).

Is there a basement?

Yes, he is.

No, there isn't.
Is the boy washing the dog?

MOVERS PRACTICE

Reading and Writing Part 1

1 Look and read. Choose the correct words and write them on the lines. There is one example.

There are two extra words that you don't need.
Check that these words don't match any of the questions!

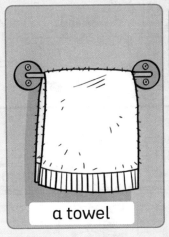

a towel

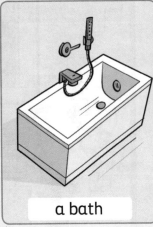

a bath

a television

a toothbrush

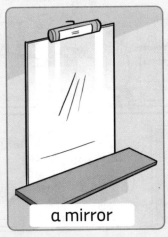

a mirror

a balcony

a lift

a clock

Example

This is an object that tells you the time.   _a clock_

Questions

1 You clean your teeth with this.   _____

2 You can go upstairs and downstairs in this.   _____

3 You can sit outside here when you live in a flat.   _____

4 You dry yourself with this after you have a shower.   _____

5 You see your face in this in the bathroom.   _____

Listening Part 2

2 🔊19 **Listen and write. There is one example.**

Read the information to find out what you need to listen for. Is it a number, a name, a person or a thing?

BUY A NEW HOME!

Type of home: _____flat_____

1 Address: 29 _____ Street

2 Floor: _____

3 You can go upstairs in: _____

4 Number of bedrooms: _____

5 You can put plants on: _____

My city

1 🔊20 **Listen. Look and point.**

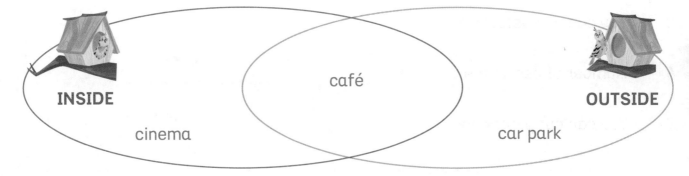

2 🔊21 **Write the numbers. Listen and check.**

café	6	hospital	☐	swimming pool	☐
car park	☐	market	☐	station	☐
cinema	☐	shopping centre	☐	sports centre	☐
library	☐	square	☐	bus station	☐

centre (UK)
center (US)

3 **Write the words.**

INSIDE

café

OUTSIDE

cinema

car park

24

4 🔊22 **Write the words. Listen and check. Then say three more types of transport.**

driver • ticket • drive • fly • catch • road • station • bus stop

driver

driver
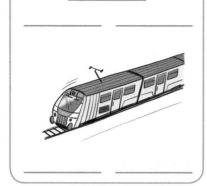

5 🔊23 **Listen and tick (✔).**

Where does Matt's mother take him?

A
B
C  ✔

1 How does Jane go to school on Fridays?

A
B
C

2 How does the man travel at work?

A
B
C

3 Which transport does the woman choose?

A
B
C

6 **Say & Play** **Choose two cards and mime.**

Are you going to the sports centre by car?

7 🔊24 **Listen and read.**

8 **Put the words in order. Then put a tick (✔) or cross (✗) in the box.**

Look & Learn

There's a big box!
There are four numbers.
Is there a cinema?

▶ *there is / there are* p. 140

there / in / a sports centre / your city? / Is
Is there a sports centre in your city?

1 city. / are / cinemas / in / There / two / my

_____ ☐

2 Are / any bus stops / your school? / there / near

_____ ☐

3 a big / is / shopping centre / in / my city. / There

_____ ☐

4 a hospital / near / There / isn't / my house.

_____ ☐

5 Are / any squares / the city centre? / in / there

_____ ☐

9 Where is Zoe? Write the words.

above · below · near · next to · opposite · between · behind · in front of

next to

1 _____

2 _____

3 _____

4 _____

5 _____

6 _____

7 _____

10 Say & Play Ask and answer questions. Write the places on the map.

Excuse me, where is the library?

The library is...

11 Say & Play Student A, look at the picture below. Student B, look at the picture on page 125. Look at the example and find four more differences.

In my picture, there's a helicopter above the hospital.

In my picture, there's a plane above the hospital.

Listening Part 3

1 **Mrs Green is telling Paul about the people in her family. Where is each person now?**

Read the question. Think about words we use to talk about the places.

Listen and write a letter in each box. There is one example.

 her sister | H |

 A

 B

 her brother | |

 her aunt | |

 C

 D

 her daughter | |

 E

 F

 her cousin | |

 her son | |

 G

 H

Reading and Writing Part 4

2 **Read the text. Choose the right words and write them on the lines.**

You don't need to think of a word – look at the three words below and choose the correct one.

A SHOPPING CENTRE

Example The Dubai Mall __is__ a huge shopping centre in Dubai,
a big city in the United Arab Emirates. You can buy books, food,
1 clothes, toys, a computer, a TV and other things _____
2 your home. _____ you hungry after shopping?
3 _____ are more than 200 cafés! Children and grown-ups
can have fun at the cinema and the zoo – it's under the water!
To get there, you can drive or catch the bus.
4 The bus stop is _____ the car park.
5 The Dubai Mall is open _____ day of the week.

Example	have	is	are
1	for	to	at
2	Have	Is	Are
3	This	They	There
4	next	near	in front
5	every	both	some

1 🔊26 **Find the words. Circle words about places in blue, the family in red, travelling in green and the home in purple. Listen and check.**

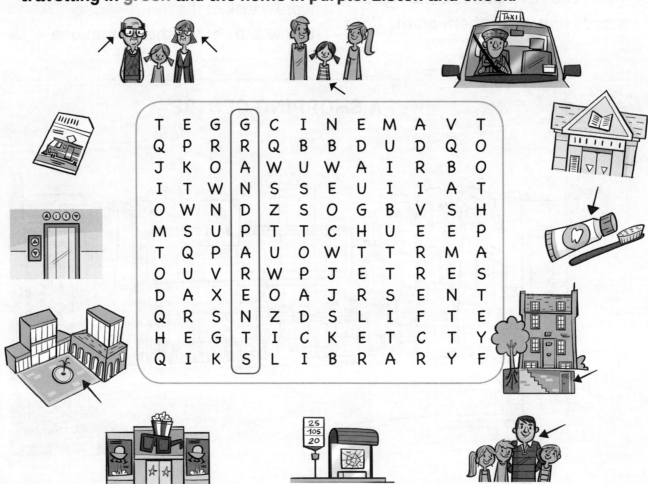

T	E	G	G	C	I	N	E	M	A	V	T
Q	P	R	R	Q	B	B	D	U	D	Q	O
J	K	O	A	W	U	W	A	I	R	B	O
I	T	W	N	S	S	E	U	I	I	A	T
O	W	N	D	Z	S	O	G	B	V	S	H
M	S	U	P	T	T	C	H	U	E	E	P
T	Q	P	A	U	O	W	T	T	R	M	A
O	U	V	R	W	P	J	E	T	R	E	S
D	A	X	E	O	A	J	R	S	E	N	T
Q	R	S	N	Z	D	S	L	I	F	T	E
H	E	G	T	I	C	K	E	T	C	T	Y
Q	I	K	S	L	I	B	R	A	R	Y	F

2 Say & Play Look at the pictures quickly. Then close your book. What are the people doing? Ask your partner.

> Number 3.

> No! He's washing his hands.

> He's doing homework.

3 ▶ **Watch the** video**. Then answer the questions.**

- Read and circle the Present simple in green and the Present continuous in blue.

> Today is Wednesday. On Wednesdays, I always ride my bike after school with my sister, Vicky. Vicky is tall and she's got long hair. She's riding the purple bike and I'm riding the blue one. Let's go!

Come into my house!

- Read and match.

1 there is/isn't   **a** ☐ things we usually do

2 Present simple   **b** ☐ things we're doing now

3 Present continuous   **c** ☐ things that are in a place

- Read and complete.

In Lucy's garden, _____ a big tree near the road.

Behind the tree, _____ two bikes: one blue and one purple.

4 Say & Play **Look at the pictures. Ask and answer questions about the story.**

A DAY AT THE SHOPPING CENTRE

Julia   Fred   Uncle Jim

5 It's a sunny day

1 🔊27 **Listen. Look and point.**

1 sun
2
3
4
5
6
7
8

2 🔊28 **Write the words. Listen and check.**

sun • clouds • rainbow • rain • moon and stars • ice • wind • snow

3 Read and complete.

Across →

3 They are white or grey.

5 Water that falls from the sky.

6 You can fly your kite in this.

7 This is big and white and is in the sky at night.

Down ↓

1 Water changes into this when it's very cold.

2 This is big and yellow and is in the sky in the day.

4 This is cold and white and you can find it on mountains.

5 It's got seven colours.

32

4 🔊29 **Listen and point. Then match and say.**

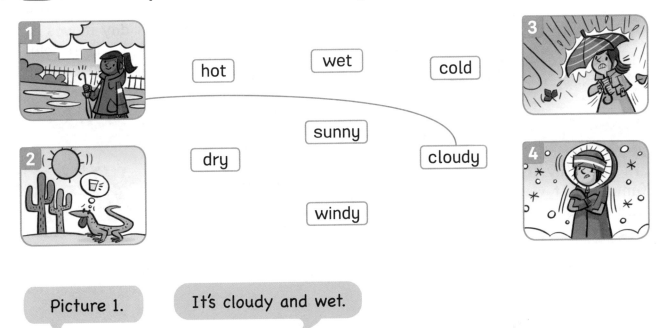

hot   wet   cold

sunny

dry   cloudy

windy

Picture 1.   It's cloudy and wet.

5 🔊30 **Say the Sounds Listen and say this three times.**

What's the weather like?
It's windy and wet.

6 **Say & Play Choose a card. Ask and answer.**

What's the weather like today?

It's cloudy. There's ice.

Look & Learn

There's ice.
It's windy.
It's snowing.

7 **Say & Play Roll the dice and tell the story.**

Five. Charlie.

One day, Charlie goes to the park...

Two. The park.

8 ◁)31 **Listen and read.**

Hi Lucy! My trip was fantastic! It was sunny and I was very happy!

Here are my friends at the swimming pool. The water was very cold!

Squawk!

My friends were there, too. The last day it was cloudy but it wasn't cold.

And here we were...

Look! It's snowing! Let's go and play!

9 ◁)32 **Read and complete. Listen and check.**

was (x 3) • What • It • wasn't like • Was • were

Look & Learn

It **was** sunny yesterday
It **wasn't** cloudy.
My friends **were** there.

▶ was / were p. 141

Sally	What __was__ the weather like on your trip last week, Nick?
Nick	The weather (**1**) _____ very good on Monday. It was cold and wet.
Sally	Oh, no! (**2**) _____ it wet all week?
Nick	No! It was OK on Wednesday. (**3**) _____ wasn't cold but it (**4**) _____ windy. Here's a picture of me flying my kite!
Sally	That looks fun! (**5**) _____ was the weather (**6**) _____ on Thursday?
Nick	It (**7**) _____ hot and sunny!
Sally	Oh, that's good!
Nick	Yes, we (**8**) _____ outside all day!

10 **Read and answer the questions.**

Hi Alex,

I'm on holiday near the beach. Today the weather isn't very good. It's wet and windy. I'm writing postcards to my friends and reading my book. Yesterday it was windy, too, but the weather was great for flying kites! On Thursday it was sunny but it was cold on the beach. There were lots of beautiful shells in the sand. I want to go and swim in the sea. I can take photos of the fish with my new camera because it can take pictures under water! Come to my house on Saturday and see my photos.

See you at the weekend,

Nick

Where is Nick on holiday? at the beach

1 What is the weather like today?

2 What was the weather like yesterday?

3 Was it hot on Thursday?

4 What does Nick want to do?

5 Where can Alex see Nick's photos?

11 **Say & Play** **Where were Lucy and Tom last week? What was the weather like? Student A, look at the table below. Student B, look at the table on page 125. Ask and answer questions.**

Monday	Tuesday	Wednesday	Thursday	Friday	Saturday	Sunday
(snowy)	**?**	(rainy)	(cloudy)	(windy)	(sunny)	(rainy)
(park)	(cinema)	(house)	**?**	(café)	(beach)	(home)

What was the weather like on Tuesday?

It was...
Where were Lucy and Tom on Wednesday?

12 **Now find three differences.**

On Monday it was snowy and they were in the park.

No, they weren't in the park. They were...

Listening Part 4

1 🔊33 **Listen and tick (✔) the box.**
There is one example.

> Read the question first.
> Listen to the end of the
> conversation before you decide!

What does Alice need?

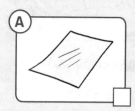 A

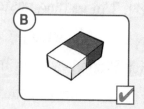 B ✔

 C

1 What was the weather like yesterday afternoon?

 A

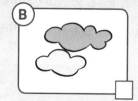 B

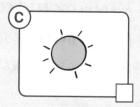 C

2 Where is Daisy going?

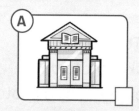 A

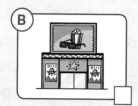 B

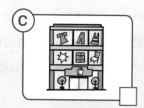 C

3 Where is Julia's homework?

 A

 B

 C

4 Who is Sam's uncle?

 A

 B

 C

5 What does May do in the basement?

 A

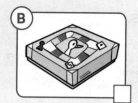 B

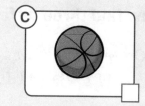 C

Reading and Writing Part 6

2 Look and read and write.

For questions 1 and 2, write between one and three words. For questions 3-6 write complete sentences. Make sure you write two different sentences for answers 5 and 6!

Examples

The cat is sleeping on __a rug__ .

What's the father wearing? __A green shirt__ .

Complete the sentences.

1   The boy on the sofa has got blond _____ .

2   The two girls are playing _____ .

Answer the questions.

3   What's the weather like?   _____ .

4   Where is the clock?   _____ .

Now write two sentences about the picture.

5   _____ .

6   _____ .

6 A shopping day

1 ◀))34 **Listen. Look and point.**

2 ◀))35 **Put the letters in the correct order. Listen and check.**

1 tah	hat	**7** nhaabdg	_____
2 aealbslb pac	_____	**8** sders	_____
3 tihsr	_____	**9** ejnsa	_____
4 kisrt	_____	**10** toosb	_____
5 cjteka	_____	**11** kssoc	_____
6 rsersuot	_____	**12** ssheo	_____

3 **Where do you wear the clothes? Write.**

🙂	👕	🩳	🧦
hat,			

4 ◀))36 **Find the clothes in the picture on page 38. Colour and write. Then listen and check.**

scarf • coat • T-shirt • helmet
sweater • swimsuit • bag

Look & Learn

a scarf ---▸ two scarves

a green T-shirt

1 _____

2 _____

3 _____

4 _____

5 _____

6 _____

5 ◀))37 **Say the Sounds Listen and say. Match the words.**

1 swimsuit   **a** her
2 shirt   **b** boot

6 ◀))38 **Listen and number. There are two pictures you do not need.**

7 **Say & Play What are you wearing? Say *yes* or *no*.**

I'm wearing blue shoes.

No, you aren't! You're wearing black shoes!

8 🔊39 **Listen and read.**

So, have you got a birthday present for Grace?

Well, first Tom wanted to buy her a book, but Grace has got a LOT of books.

Then we went to the clothes shop. I saw some beautiful T-shirts! But then Tom had a great idea.

And... ?

Well, Grace told him that her mum and dad are getting her a new bike and...

So... ?

So we bought her a new helmet!

Oh... Zoe!

9 🔊40 **Write the verbs. Listen and check.**

> ~~told~~ • drank • bought • had • looked • wanted • saw • ate
> went • needed • liked • opened • found • got

Regular verbs (verb + -ed)	Irregular verbs
_____	told, _____
_____	_____
_____	_____

Look & Learn

look ---➤ look**ed** (regular)
tell ---➤ **told** (irregular)

▶ Past simple p. 141

10 Read and complete.

Lucy and Tom __went__ (go) shopping.

1 They _____ (buy) a present for Grace.

2 Tom _____ (want) to buy Grace a book.

3 Tom _____ (drink) his milkshake.

4 Zoe _____ (open) the box.

5 They all _____ (like) the helmet.

11 Read the story. Then complete the sentences with 1, 2 or 3 words.

A Shopping Day

Bill lives with his parents in a village. Last Saturday Bill's grandmother took him to a new shopping centre to buy a toy. The shopping centre was very big and there were lots of different kinds of shops. It was very busy and there were a lot of people. 'I don't like this shopping centre', Bill said. 'I can't find the shop I want to go to.' 'Here's a map,' Bill's grandmother said. But Bill wasn't happy. 'I'm tired and I'm hungry!', he said. 'I want to go home.' Bill's grandmother drove back to the village. When they got there, she gave Bill a small bag. When he opened the bag, he found the new computer game he wanted.
'Oh, thank you, Grandma! You're brilliant!'

Bill's house is in ___a village___ .

1 Bill went shopping with
   _____.

2 Bill wanted to buy _____.

3 Bill wanted to go home because
   he _____.

4 Bill's grandmother gave him
   _____ when they were
   in the village.

5 There was a _____ inside
   the bag.

12 Now tell the story using your words and the verbs in the box.

is • go • buy • live • say • drive • give

Bill lives with his parents in a village.

One day, he went...

13 Write three sentences about you.

I	eat (a pizza) play (football) go (to the park) buy (a computer game) see (my friends)	yesterday last weekend on (Saturday)

I went to the cinema yesterday.

Listening Part 1

1 🔊41 **Listen and draw lines. There is one example.**

Paul   Jill   Alice

Read the names and think: are they boys or girls? Then listen and find the person. What's his/her name?

Ben   May   Matt   Pat

Reading and Writing Part 3

2 **Read the story. Choose a word from the box.
Write the correct word next to numbers 1-5.
There is one example.**

> Read the story first. Then look at the words before and after the spaces.

Alex and Kim live in the city. They sometimes ride their bikes at the weekend.
Last Sunday they went to a big <u>park</u> .
It was a **(1)** _____ day and they put on their coats, scarves and hats.
The wind was behind them and they **(2)** _____ their bikes quickly.
Alex lost his **(3)** _____ in the wind. 'Where is it?', he said.
Then he saw it. It was in a **(4)** _____. 'How can we get it down?',
Alex said. Then, Kim had an idea. 'I can climb the tree,' she said.
Kim put on her helmet and started to climb. She picked up the scarf and put it
around her **(5)** _____. Then she climbed down. 'Thank you, Kim!',
Alex said. 'You're very brave!'

Example		
park	tree	neck
sun	rode	foot
scarf	cold	drove

(6) Now choose the best name for the story. Tick one box.

A rainy day ☐   Alex's favourite scarf ☐   A good friend ☐

 **Lucy's birthday party**

1 🔊 42 **Listen. Look and point.**

film star (UK)

movie star (US)

2 🔊 43 **Write the numbers. Listen and check.**

pirate 4	doctor ☐	driver ☐	farmer ☐	film star ☐
pop star ☐	clown ☐	dentist ☐	nurse ☐	cook ☐

3 **Read and write the words.**

I take you and your friends to school every day. _____driver_____

1 You can see me on television or at the cinema. _____

2 I look inside your mouth to see your teeth. _____

3 I make food in a café. _____

4 You can see me at the circus. _____

5 I sing songs and make music videos. _____

6 I grow food and feed my animals. _____

7 You come to see me when you aren't well. _____

8 I work in the hospital with the doctor. _____

9 I go on my boat and look for treasure. _____

4 Look and write.

plate(s) · cup(s) · glass(es) · bottle(s) · bowl(s) · box(es)

There is a _bowl_ of grapes.

1 There is a _____ of chocolates.

2 There is a _____ of lemonade.

3 There are four _____ of juice.

4 There are three _____ of ice cream.

5 There are two _____ of tea.

6 There is a _____ of fruit.

5 Write the food and drinks in the bottle, the plate, the bowl or the cup.

chips · sausages · eggs · water · coffee · fish · hot chocolate
lemonade · beans · chicken · milk · meatballs · rice · meat

water

sausages

chips

coffee

6 Say & Play Choose a card and play. Guess the word.

It's a person. He's got lots of animals and he grows vegetables.

It's a farmer! My turn. It's a thing. You put food on it...

7 Lucy's birthday party

7 🔊44 **Listen and read.**

Hi Tom! Do you want some birthday cake?

Yes, please. I didn't eat any at your party.

Did you enjoy the party? You looked like a famous pop star!

Yes, I did. It was fun.

And Charlie's clothes were fantastic, too! When I saw him, I thought he was a real cook!

You mean... that cake!

Yes, and he made this cake.

Look & Learn

I **didn't eat** the cake.
Did you **enjoy** the party?
Yes, I **did**. / No, I **didn't**.

▶ Past simple p. 141

8 🔊45 **Read and complete. Listen and check.**

Mary	Happy birthday, Lucy! I'm sorry I <u>didn't come</u> (not come) to your party.
Lucy	Hi, Grandma! That's OK.
Mary	**(1)** _____ (you / enjoy) the party?
Lucy	Yes, I **(2)** _____! My friends dressed up in great clothes.
Mary	What **(3)** _____ (you / wear)?
Lucy	I wore a scarf, a shirt and some old trousers.
Mary	**(4)** _____ (you / dress up) as a farmer?
Lucy	No, I **(5)** _____! I was a pirate!

46

9 Look again at the picture on page 44. Write about Lucy's party.

pop star / wear / a hat   The pop star didn't wear a hat.

1 clown / have / a green nose   _____

2 cook / make / meatballs   _____

3 doctor / wear / white coat   _____

4 driver / drive / a bus   _____

5 film star / wear / a sweater   _____

6 nurse / eat / ice cream   _____

10 Think about a birthday party. Then ask and answer questions.

1 Where / you / have the party?   **4** What games / you / play?

2 What / you / eat?   **5** What / you / wear?

3 What / you / drink?   **6** What / your friends / wear?

> Where did you have the party?

> I had the party in the park.

11 ◀))46 Listen and tick (✔).

1 What did the girl do after her homework?

A    B    C

2 Where did the woman go when it started to rain?

A   B    C

3 What did the boy find?

A   B    C

12 Say & Play Write three sentences about last weekend. Play _True or False_?

> I didn't go to the market on Saturday.

> I think it's true.

> No, it's false! I went to the market!

MOVERS PRACTICE

Reading and Writing Part 5

1 **Look at the pictures and read the story. Write some words to complete the sentences about the story. You can use 1, 2 or 3 words.**

> The pictures don't give you the answers! You need to read and understand the story.

JILL'S HOMEWORK

Jill goes to a big school in the city. Last Friday, her teacher, Mr Brown, said 'For your homework, please write about someone's work.' Jill thought about her homework all day but she didn't write a word. Jill's mum saw her sad face. 'What's the matter, Jill?' said her mum. 'I can't do my homework,' said Jill. 'I don't know what to write.'

Examples

Jill's school is __in the city__ .   Jill's teacher is called __Mr Brown__ .

Questions

1 Jill had to write about someone's work for _____.

2 Jill was _____ because she didn't know what to write.

On Saturday morning, Jill's dad put on his white coat and smiled. 'Eat your breakfast, then come with me,' he said. Jill's dad works at the hospital. He took Jill there and she watched the doctors and nurses work. Jill asked a lot of questions and she drew pictures in her book.

3 Jill's dad put on _____ on Saturday morning.

4 Jill's dad took her to _____.

5 Jill _____ of the doctors and nurses in her book.

Then, Jill saw a young woman who couldn't walk. She had a pink hat on her head and Jill couldn't see her face. Jill helped her sit down. 'Thank you,' said the woman and she looked at Jill. It was her favourite pop star! Jill's dad took a photo of them. 'I'm very happy!' Jill said. 'And now I have something to write about for my homework!'

6 The woman said _____ because Jill helped her.

7 Jill was happy because she saw her_____.

Speaking Part 2

2 🔊**47 Listen and tell the story.**

PAT GOES TO A PARTY

Look at the pictures and think about the story. Then think of words to talk about the things you see.

Pat

1

2

3

4

3 ▶ **Now watch the video and talk about your answers.**

8 Our beautiful world

1 ◀))48 **Listen. Look and point.**

1 forest
2
3
4
5
6
7
8
9
10

2 ◀))49 **Write the words. Listen and check.**

village • sea • fields • ~~forest~~
road • river • mountain
lake • waterfall • beach

3 ◀))50 **Say the Sounds Listen. Which are the letters you don't hear? Circle.**

1 i s l a n d
2 t w o
3 l i s t e n
4 s c h o o l

4 **Look and write.**

Which places have got water?
waterfall,
Where do animals live?

5 🔊**51** **Listen and look at Tom's photos. Where did he take them?**

Look & Learn

a lea**f** ---➤ some
                    lea**ves**

1 near a _mountain_
2 in a _____
3 in a _____
4 on a _____
5 by the _____

6 **Student A, look below. Student B, go to page 126. Listen and draw.**

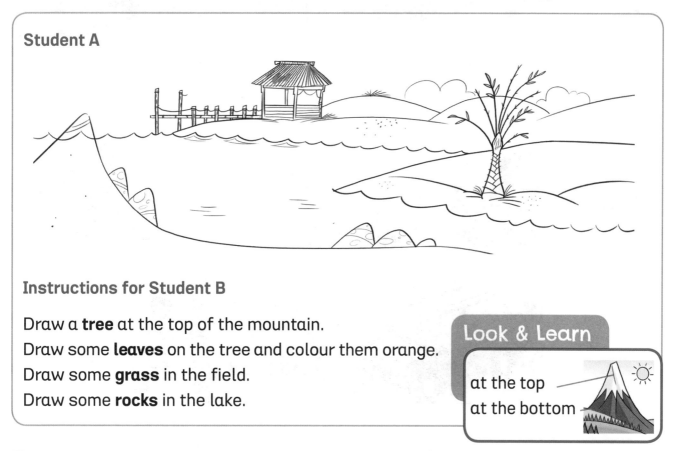

Student A

Instructions for Student B

Draw a **tree** at the top of the mountain.
Draw some **leaves** on the tree and colour them orange.
Draw some **grass** in the field.
Draw some **rocks** in the lake.

Look & Learn

at the top
at the bottom

7 **Say & Play Draw a map of your island. Then tell your partner about it.**

On my island, there's a forest in front of a mountain. There are lots of tall trees.

51

8 🔊52 **Listen and read.**

Do you want to come to the countryside? We can go for a walk in the forest.

No thanks, Tom. I don't like going to the countryside.

I love swimming at the beach.

There's a river and a waterfall.

And can we go for a swim there?

Well... Yes!

OK, Tom. Yes, I'd like to come!

Fantastic!

Look & Learn

We can **go for a walk**.

9 **Look and match.**

d

1

2

3

4

| **a** | go for a drive | **b** | go for an ice cream | **c** | go for a bike ride |

| **d** | go for a walk | **e** | go for a swim |

10 Read and complete.

> to go for a walk • ~~going~~ • to take
> eating • to go for a swim • looking

Tom enjoys __going__ to the countryside.

1 Tom wants _____ in the forest.
2 He wants _____ photos of plants and flowers.
3 Lucy wants _____ in the sea.
4 She doesn't enjoy _____ at plants.
5 Tom and Lucy like _____ ice cream.

11 🔊53 Listen to Ben and tick (✔) or cross (✘).

Paul		✘		✔	✔
Sally					
Jim					
May					

12 Say & Play Describe a person from exercise 11. Who is he/she?

> This person likes walking in the mountains. Who is it?

> Is it Sally?

13 What do people in your class like doing? Write activities and places. Then ask and answer questions and complete.

	swimming in rivers	
Sue	✘	

> Do you enjoy swimming in rivers, Sue?

> No, I don't. I like going for a swim at the beach.

Reading and Writing Part 2

1 Read the text and choose the best answer.

Example

Kim Hi, Nick. What did you do at the weekend?

Nick A I'm going to the cinema.
B I went to the cinema.
C I go to the cinema on Fridays.

> Read all the answers before you choose.
> Look at words like *his, her, it*.
> What are they talking about?

Questions

1 Kim Did you see the film about the island?
Nick A Yes, I loved it!
B Yes, I went there.
C Yes, I saw her, too.

2 Kim My favourite part was when the girl got to the top of the mountain.
Nick A The mountain was tall.
B No, she didn't.
C I liked that part, too.

3 Kim Do you like going to the mountains?
Nick A Yes, I enjoy going for walks there.
B Yes, I would like to go.
C That's a good idea.

4 Kim Last year I went for a swim in the lake.
Nick A Do you?
B I can't swim.
C Was it fun?

5 Kim Yes! Would you like to come with me at the weekend?
Nick A Thank you, but I'm busy.
B I couldn't go on Saturday.
C Yes, I'm going on holiday.

6 Kim OK. Shall we do something this afternoon?
Nick A Yes, I did my homework.
B Let's go for an ice cream!
C I'm in the countryside.

Speaking Part 1

2 🔊54 **Listen and find the differences.**

Say what the people are doing in each picture. Use *In this picture, a girl is... + -ing.*

A

B

3 ▶ **Now watch the video and talk about your answers.**

1 **What's wrong? Find four more mistakes.**

The rainbow has got three colours: red, white and orange.

2 **Find the words. Which words are different?**

1 _____   2 _____   3 _____

3 ▶ **Watch the** video**. Then answer the questions.**

- Complete the table.

PAST SIMPLE			
Affirmative (+)		**Negative (-)**	
It ___was___ sunny.		It _____ sunny.	
I _____ to school.		I _____ go to school.	
He _____ ice cream.		He _____ eat ice cream.	
They _____ a mountain.		They _____ climb a mountain.	
Questions		**Answers**	
_____ it sunny?		Yes, it _____.	
Did you _____ to school?		No, I _____.	
_____ he _____ ice cream?		No, he _____.	
_____ they _____ a mountain?		Yes, they _____.	

A day in the countryside

- Circle the correct words.

1 I want to **go** / **going** for a walk.
2 I like **eat** / **eating** chocolate.
3 I don't like **swim** / **swimming** in the sea.
4 I would like to **be** / **being** in the park today.

4 **Say & Play What did you do last Saturday? Choose and guess.**

Did you go for a swim?

Yes, I did.

9 At the farm

1 🔊55 **Listen. Look and point.**

2 🔊56 **Look, find and write. Listen and check.**

goat • chicken • cow • donkey • duck • fly
horse • kitten • sheep • parrot • puppy • rabbit

Look & Learn

Look at that **fly**!
(noun)
The duck is trying to **fly**.
(verb)

puppy

 1 _____

 2 _____

3 _____

4 _____

5 _____

 6 _____

7 _____

8 _____

9 _____

10 _____

11 _____

3 🔊57 **Say the Sounds Listen and say.**

The **n**aughty **h**orse is drawing on the **w**all.

58

4 Look at the pictures and say which one is different.

A duck, a chicken and a parrot are birds. A kitten isn't a bird.

5 🔊58 **Look and circle. Listen and check.**

The horse is (huge) / small.
1 The cat is **naughty** / **good**.
2 The parrot is **silly** / **clever**.
3 The puppy is **small** / **big**.
4 The horse is **strong** / **weak**.
5 The cat is **thirsty** / **hungry**.
6 The parrot is **ugly** / **pretty**.
7 The puppy is **asleep** / **awake**.

6 Say & Play Which animal is it? Ask and answer questions.

7 🔊59 **Listen and read.**

Which animal did you like at the farm, Tom?

I don't know. I liked all the animals.

The horse was the biggest.

Yes, it was huge! And it was stronger than the other animals.

The kittens were nice. They were smaller than the puppies.

But the puppies were prettier! And what's the cleverest animal, Lucy?

That's easy! The cleverest animal is...

Zoe! Zoe! Zoe!

▶ **Comparatives and Superlatives p. 141**

8 **Read and write *yes* or *no*.**

Horses are bigger than donkeys. <u>yes</u>

1 Kittens are older than cats. ____

2 Horses are stronger than frogs. ____

3 Birds are smaller than bees. ____

4 Puppies are younger than dogs. ____

5 Parrots are prettier than cows. ____

9 **Write sentences. Then read about the animals on page 61 and write *True* or *False*.**

Flies / small / parrots   Flies are smaller than parrots.   True

1 Horses / strong / donkeys _____ _____

2 Donkeys / big / parrots _____ _____

3 Parrots / slow / flies _____ _____

4 Donkeys / quick / animal _____ _____

5 Parrots / clever / bird _____ _____

Donkeys

Colours: white, brown, grey or black

How big? 125 cm (foot to shoulder)   **Food:** grass

Did you know?

- Donkeys are strong animals – they are stronger than horses!
- They can run at 50 km an hour.
- Donkeys are also clever and they like living with other donkeys.
- Donkeys don't like the rain!

Parrots

Colours: many different colours

How big? between 8 cm and 100 cm

Food: flower seeds

Did you know?

- Parrots can fly at 24 km an hour.
- Parrots are cleverer than all other birds.
- Some parrots can live for more than 80 years!
- The most famous parrot was called Alex!

Flies

Colours: brown or black

How big? smaller than 1.5 cm

Food: our food and drinks

Did you know?

- Flies haven't got teeth.
- Flies have got huge eyes and they can see behind them!
- They can fly at 7 km an hour for a short time.
- Flies can walk on walls and they can walk upside down!

10 **Which animal do you think is the best? Draw and write. Compare it with other animals.**

11 **Choose and talk about the best farm animals.**

Which animal is the quickest?

Cows are quicker than sheep.

But horses are quicker than cows. They're the quickest animal on the farm.

Best animals on the farm

The quickest animal   _____

The prettiest animal   _____

The strongest animal   _____

The cleverest animal   _____

The funniest animal   _____

MOVERS PRACTICE

Reading and Writing Part 1

1 **Look and read. Choose the correct words and write them on the lines. There is one example.**

Write the correct spelling of the words!

a field

a river

a rabbit

a forest

a kitten

grass

a market

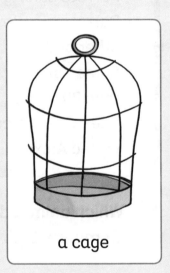

a cage

Example

Some people put their birds or rabbits inside this. _____a cage_____

Questions

1 This is a young animal. It is often a pet. _____

2 Horses and cows like eating this. It's green. _____

3 You can buy fruit and vegetables here. _____

4 Farmers grow vegetables and other plants here. _____

5 This animal lives under the ground. _____

Listening Part 5

2 🔊60 **Listen and colour and write.**
There is one example.

Only colour the things you hear. Don't colour other things in the picture!

10 The animal park

1 🔊61 **Listen. Look and point.**

2 🔊62 **Write the words. Listen and check.**

1 <u>penguin</u>

2 _____   6 _____

3 _____   7 _____

4 _____   8 _____

5 _____   9 _____

> bat • dolphin • kangaroo
> lion • panda • ~~penguin~~
> shark • snail • whale

3 **Look and write the animals in their homes.**

4 **Now write more words in exercise 3.**

penguin

> bear • spider • monkey
> zebra • polar bear
> snake • giraffe • tiger
> crocodile • hippo
> elephant • fish

5 Look at the pictures. Circle the words that you think are in the story.

quietly · quickly · loud · slowly · surprised · carefully · dangerous
beautiful · wet · well · terrible · hungry

6 ◀))63 Put the pictures in order. Listen and check.

7 ◀))63 Listen again and circle (A or B). Then tell the story.

The woman told the children
not to go...
  A to their seats.
  B near the water.

1 The woman told the children not
to speak loudly because...
  A dolphins are afraid of loud noises.
  B people couldn't hear
the music.

2 The boy thought the dolphins...
  A swam very well.
  B jumped very well.

3 The girl wanted to give
the dolphins fish because...
  A the boy asked her to feed
them.
  B she thought they were hungry.

4 The girl was wet because...
  A she jumped into the water.
  B a dolphin jumped into the water.

5 The girl was surprised because
the dolphin...
  A jumped quickly.
  B jumped quietly.

8 Say & Play Choose a card and play the game. What's the animal?

Does it run quickly?

Yes, it does.

Is it black and white?

No, it isn't.

9 🔊64 **Listen and read.**

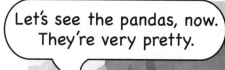

Let's see the pandas, now. They're very pretty.

Yes, they're more beautiful than the bats!

I think the kangaroos are more dangerous than that lion.

Yes, they can kick you with their strong legs.

These penguins are the best parents in the animal park.

Crocodiles are more careful than penguins. They carry their babies in their mouths!

Hmm, I like this snake. I'd love a pet snake.

No, Tom. Parrots are the best pets.

Look & Learn

good ---→ better ---→ the best
bad ---→ worse ---→ the worst

▶ **Comparatives and Superlatives p. 141**

10 **Write sentences.**

pandas / beautiful / bats
Pandas are more beautiful than bats.

1 kangaroos / dangerous / lions

_____

2 crocodiles / careful / penguins

_____

3 penguins / good / parents

_____

4 snakes / bad / pets

_____

11 **What's your favourite animal? Say why.**

My favourite animal is the parrot. They are prettier than other birds.

Yes, I think they are the prettiest birds in the world.

12 Look and match.

The horse is skating

1 The crocodile is swimming
2 The panda is listening to music
3 The kangaroo is playing basketball
4 The penguin is painting
5 The polar bear is eating

a better than Mark.
b more slowly than Alice.
c worse than Bill.
d more carefully than Nick.
e more quickly than Sam.
f more quietly than Sally.

13 Look and talk about Eva and Jim.

Eva is running more quickly than Jim. / Jim is running more slowly than Eva.

Reading and Writing Part 4

1 **Read the text. Choose the right words and write them on the lines.**

> Read the words before and after the space. Sometimes these words help you choose the right word.

PENGUINS

Example	Penguins are birds that live __in__ very cold places.
	Their black and white colours help them hide from whales or sharks
1	when they're _____ in the sea.
2	Penguins live with _____ families. When the penguin
3	mother _____ fishing, the father carefully puts
	the egg on his feet, under his body.
4	Penguins can swim very _____. They jump in and
5	out of the water when they want to go more _____.

Example	in	for	on
1	swam	swim	swimming
2	her	their	your
3	go	goes	going
4	well	good	best
5	quick	quicker	quickly

Speaking Part 3

2 🔊65 **Listen and say which one is different.**

Talk about each picture in a short sentence.

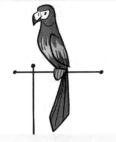

Speaking Part 4

3 **Ask and answer the questions with your partner.**

1 How many people are there in your family?

2 Who are they?

3 What do you like doing with your family?

4 Where do you like going at the weekend with your family?

5 Where do you live?

6 Have you got any pets? What are their names?

Listen for the question words *What? Which? Where? When? Who? How? How many? How often?* and *Why?*

4 ▶ **Now watch the video and talk about your answers.**

At the sports centre

1 🔊66 **Listen. Look and point.**

2 🔊67 **Write the words. Listen and check.**

> run • skip • score • hit • climb • skate • jump • kick • bounce • hop

1 hit _____ **6** _____

2 _____ **7** _____

3 _____ **8** _____

4 _____ **9** _____

5 _____ **10** _____

Look & Learn

I **practise** climbing every day. (verb)
I go to basketball **practice**. (noun)

3 **Tick (✔) the sports you can see in the picture.**

badminton	☐	skateboarding	☐	baseball	☐
tennis	☐	ice skating	☐	hockey	☐
roller skating	☐	football	☐	table tennis	☐

4 🔊68 **What do you do in each sport? Write. Listen and check.**

You play badminton with a shuttlecock.

Football	Hockey	Basketball	Badminton
run,	run,	run,	run,

5 **Find these things in the picture on page 70. Then write the words.**

eic tsseka   _ice skates_

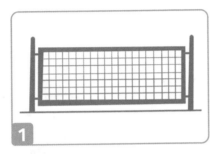

1   ent _____

2   lpayre _____

3   elrorl assket _____

4   kaetrc _____

5   sabtdrkoae _____

6 **Say & Play** **Play *What am I doing?* Choose a sport and mime.**

Are you hitting a ball?

7 🔊**69** **Listen and read.**

In basketball you mustn't walk or run with the ball.

You must bounce the ball with one hand. You must play inside the lines.

You mustn't kick the ball. Now, who wants to play?

Me! Me!

Zoe wants to play, too!

Look & Learn

You **must** bounce the ball.
You **mustn't** kick the ball.
What **must**/**mustn't** you do?

▶ *must* p. 142

8 **How do you play basketball?**
Read and colour.

You must...

You mustn't...

kick the ball

walk with the ball

go outside the lines

put the ball in the net to score

run and jump

bounce the ball

9 🔊**70** **Say the Sounds Listen and say.**
Circle the letter you don't hear.

You **m u s t n ' t** fly with the ball!

10 Look, read and complete with *must* or *mustn't*.

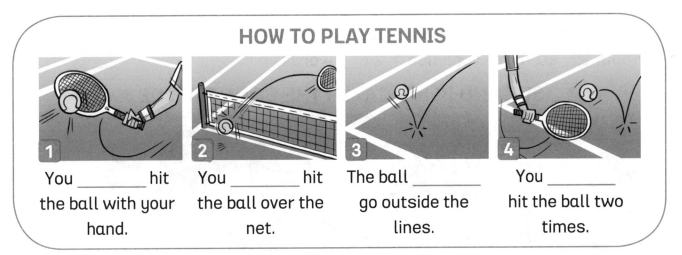

HOW TO PLAY TENNIS

1 You _____ hit the ball with your hand.

2 You _____ hit the ball over the net.

3 The ball _____ go outside the lines.

4 You _____ hit the ball two times.

11 ◀)71 Listen and tick (✔) or cross (✗).

AT THE SWIMMING POOL

1 2 3 4
5 6 7 8

12 Ask and answer the questions. Write your partner's answers.

1 What sports do you play?

2 What is your favourite sport?

3 Where do you play it?

4 What do you wear?

5 What must you do?

6 What mustn't you do?

13 Say & Play Talk about another sport. Don't say the sport!

In this sport you must run. You don't wear a helmet. You score goals.

Is it football?

MOVERS PRACTICE

Reading and Writing Part 5

1 **Look at the pictures and read the story. Write some words to complete the sentences about the story. You can use 1, 2 or 3 words.**

> Read the sentence and think about the words you need to complete it.

SUE AND BEN'S DAY IN THE COUNTRYSIDE

Sue's family lived in a city but in the holidays she and her brother, Ben, always went to her aunt and uncle's house in the countryside. 'I love going to Aunt Daisy's house,' said Sue in the car. 'I can play outside in the fields all day!' But when they got there, it was very cold and there was snow on the ground.

Examples

In the holidays, Sue and her brother go to <u>the countryside</u> .
They stay at their <u>aunt and uncle</u> 's house.

Questions

1 At her aunt's house, Sue loves playing in _____ .

2 Sue and Ben couldn't play outside because it _____ .

The next day, Sue picked up her ice skates. 'Come on, Ben!' she said. 'Let's go ice skating!' At the lake, Sue put on her ice skates and went onto the ice. 'Ben, come and skate with me!' she shouted. But Ben didn't want to skate, he was afraid. Sue skated happily. Then, she fell. 'Ben, my leg hurts!' she shouted. Ben ran to get help. He found a farmer who carried Sue to his tractor.

3 Sue wanted to _____ on the lake.

4 Ben didn't skate with Sue because he _____ .

5 A farmer picked Sue up and took her to _____ .

When the farmer drove Sue and Ben to their aunt's house in his tractor, she was very surprised. She was angry, too. 'You mustn't skate on the lake, Sue. It's dangerous!' she said. 'I'm sorry, Aunt Daisy!' said Sue. Then they all had tea and cake and watched a film on the sofa.

6 Sue's aunt was _____ because Sue and Ben were on a tractor.

7 She told Sue that it was _____ to skate on the lake.

Listening Part 2

2 🔊72 **Listen and write. There is one example.**

> When you have to write a name, the speaker spells the letters. Listen carefully and write the letters you hear.

THE SPORTS CENTRE

	Opposite there is:	_____a bus stop_____
1	Name of the sports centre:	_____ Sports Centre
2	Number of days open:	_____ days a week
3	Outside you can play:	football and _____
4	Kind of lessons you can have:	_____
5	Skate park next to:	_____

1 🔊73 **Listen. Look and point.**

2 🔊74 **Read and complete. Listen and check.**

> stomach-ache • cough • hurts • toothache • cold
> earache • ill • temperature • headache • fine

1 Tom's leg _hurts_ .

2 The girl has got _____.

3 The little girl's dad is _____.

4 The little girl is _____.

5 The baby has got a _____.

6 The boy has got _____.

7 The man in the red jacket has got _____.

8 The old man has got a _____.

9 The woman wearing jeans and a purple coat has got a _____.

10 The old woman has got a _____.

3 🔊75 **Say the Sounds Listen and write the words. Say.**

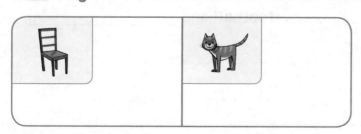

> **cheese** • **toothache** • **watch**
> **stomach-ache** • **headache**
> **lunch** • **earache**

4 🔊76 **Look at Tom and write the numbers. Listen and check.**

back	☐	leg	☐
shoulder	☐	hand	☐
neck	☐	eye	☐
stomach	☐	ear	☐
teeth	☐	mouth	☐
arm	☐	head	1
foot	☐	nose	☐

5 🔊77 **Listen to the people and tick (✔).**

1 A ☐ B ☐ C ☐

2 A ☐ B ☐ C ☐

3 A ☐ B ☐ C ☐

Look & Learn

one foot ---➤ two **feet**

one tooth ---➤ lots of **teeth**

6 Say & Play **What's the matter? Student A, look at this picture. Student B, look at the picture on page 126. Find six differences.**

Number 2. Her arm hurts.

It's different. In my picture her leg hurts.

7 ◀))78 **Listen and read.**

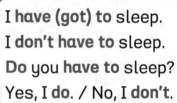

Look & Learn

I **have (got) to** sleep.
I **don't have to** sleep.
Do you **have to** sleep?
Yes, I **do.** / No, I **don't.**

▶ *have to* p. 142

8 **Lucy is better today. Read and match.**
Write *has to* or *doesn't have to*.

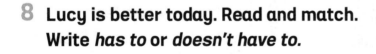

She ___has to___ write a story for homework.

1 Lucy _____ feed Zoe.

2 She _____ walk to school.

3 She _____ go to school.

4 She _____ make lunch.

5 She _____ go to bed in the afternoon.

9 🔊79 **Read, listen and complete.**

Your Homework Today

You <u>have to</u> write a story.

Your story (1) _____ be in English. Your story (2) _____ be long. You have to write (3) _____ page.

Write any kind of story: funny or scary. You (4) _____ draw pictures.

You can work with (5) _____.

You have (6) _____ your story to the class.
---

10 **Read and answer. Then ask and answer the questions.**

1 Do you have to walk to school? _____
2 Do you have to feed or take a pet for a walk? _____
3 Do you have to read books in English? _____
4 Do you have to clean your bedroom? _____
5 Do you have to help your parents at home? _____
6 Do you have to do your homework when you are ill? _____

11 **Say & Play Student A, look at the table below. Student B, look at the table on page 127. Ask and answer and tick (✔) or cross (✗).**

	go to bed	drink water	put on a hat	put ice on	put a hot towel on
	✗	✗	✔	✗	✔
	✗	✗	✗	✔	✗

I've got earache.

No, I don't. I have to put on a hat.

Do you have to go to bed?

79

Listening Part 3

1 🔊80 **The doctor is talking about the people who come to see her at work. What's the matter with each person? Listen and write a letter in each box. There is one example.**

Listen and find the person. Then listen carefully and choose the correct answer.

teacher [H]

farmer [ ]

clown [ ]

movie star [ ]

cook [ ]

driver [ ]

Speaking Part 2

2 (81) **Listen and tell the story.**

ANNA GOES TO HOSPITAL

Think carefully about the pictures. Then say what the people are doing.

3 ▶ **Now watch the video and talk about your answers.**

1 Read and write.

ACROSS →

1 This animal lives in the sea and has got big teeth.

4 You wear them on your feet when you go skating.

7 This animal has got strong legs and it can jump very well.

8 Sometimes children do things that are bad. They're...

9 This part of your body is between your arm and your neck.

DOWN ↓

2 This is a baby cat.

3 I'm not strong, I'm...

5 You can get this when you eat a lot of chocolate and sweets.

6 It's a huge animal that lives in the sea.

2 Read and complete the messages.

1 I dance, s k ● t ▲ and jump on ice. Sometimes I f ● l l .

I'm __ __ __ - __ __ __ __ __ __ __ __ .

2 I've got a c ✳ ♥ gh, a c ✳ l d and a t ▲ m p ▲ r ● t ♥ r ▲ .

I'm __ __ __ !

3 He needs to p r ● c t ■ s ▲ kicking to s c ✳ r ▲ more g ✳ ● l s .

He plays __ __ __ __ __ __ __ __ __ .

4 It's ● s l ▲ ▲ p in the day and it's ● w ● k ▲ at night.

It's c l ▲ v ▲ r but it isn't very p r ▲ t t y.

It's a __ __ __ .

3 ▶ **Watch the** video**. Then answer the questions.**

The funniest pet

• Write sentences.

1 pandas / big / penguins
2 sharks / dangerous / dolphins
3 Zoe / good / pet
4 donkeys / strong / animals / a farm
5 Lucy / sings / loudly / Tom

• Read and circle.

1 At school we **must / mustn't** listen to the teacher.
2 In football you **must / mustn't** kick other players.
3 You **have to / don't have to** do what the doctor says when you're ill.
4 Do you **must / have to** do homework every day?

4 **Say & Play** **Look at the picture. Ask and answer questions.**

13 At the funfair

1 🔊82 **Listen. Look and point.**

1 ride
2
3
4
5
6
7
8

2 🔊83 **Write the words. Listen and check.**

> throw • wave • drop • sail • fish • ride • fall • catch

3 **Look at the picture. Read and complete.**

> fishing • dropping • riding • sailing • falling • catching • waving • throwing

The man with orange hair is <u>catching</u> a green ball and he's _____ a blue ball.

1 Grace is _____ a pink horse.

2 Jack is _____ a boat.

3 Charlie is _____ at Lucy and Tom.

4 Tom is good at _____.

5 The clown is _____ the coconuts.

6 The clown can't skate. He's _____ over.

4 Answer the questions. Then talk with a partner.

Name:

1 two things you can ride _____ _____
2 something you sometimes drop _____
3 a sport where you throw and catch _____
4 a part of the body you hurt when you fall _____
5 a place where you can sail or fish _____
6 a person you wave to _____

5 🔊84 Say the Sounds Listen and say.

three   throw   **fr**uit   **fr**iend   **fr**og

Three **fr**iends **th**rowing **fr**uit at a **fr**og!

6 Who says this? Look at the picture on page 84. Read and match.

1 Charlie is very **brave**. We're up in the sky but he isn't afraid.

2 Fishing is **easy**! I've got ten ducks!

3 Ahh! Rollerskating is **dangerous**!

4 Throwing and catching five balls is **difficult**.

5 My sister is **frightened**!

6 This ride is **safe** for small children.

A ☐   B ☐

C ☐   D [1]

E ☐   F ☐

7 Say & Play You are at the funfair. Choose three things to do.

I want to... • I'd like to... • Do you want to...? • Would you like to...?
I like/don't like... • Let's....

I want to go on this ride.

I don't like sailing. It's very difficult!
Let's play this game.

OK. Let's sail in a boat.

8 ◀))85 **Listen and read.**

Can you skate, Lucy?

Yes, I can. I could skate when I was six.

The yellow clown can't skate very quickly!

No, she can't catch the red clown!

And she can't walk very well. She's falling!

Look out, Tom!

But she can throw well.

Take a photo!

Look & Learn

I **can** skate. (now)
I **couldn't** skate last year.
(in the past)

▶ *could* p. 142

9 **Read and circle.**

The red clown (could)/ **couldn't** skate well.

1 The yellow clown **could** / **couldn't** skate quickly.
2 The yellow clown wanted to **catch** / **throw** the red clown.
3 The yellow clown **could** / **couldn't** walk well.

4 The yellow clown **could** / **couldn't** throw very well.
5 Zoe asked Lucy to take a photo of **the clown** / **Tom**.

10 **Write five things you can do now. Could you do them when you were younger? Write the age you learnt to do them. Then ask and answer.**

I can... / Age
ride a bike   6
...   ...
...   ...

Can you ride a bike?

Yes, I can.

Could you ride a bike when you were three?

No, I couldn't.

11 Read. Then complete the sentences.

Hi, I'm Alex.

Last weekend I went to a circus school. It was a lot of fun! First, we learnt how to climb and jump. I'm not very good at climbing and I fell three times! I didn't hurt myself because there was a net below me. After that, the teacher wanted me to throw and catch three balls at the same time. I'm good at baseball but this was very difficult! Then, the teacher said, 'Now put on these clothes'. I wore a big orange hat, purple trousers and a red nose. Then she asked me to paint my face. 'You're very good at painting!' she said. 'Now you're a real clown!'

painting · climbing · baseball · throw · paint · wear

Alex isn't very good at _climbing_.
1 The teacher wanted Alex to _____ and catch the balls.
2 Alex is good at _____.
3 The teacher wanted Alex to _____ some funny clothes.
4 The teacher asked Alex to _____ his face.
5 The teacher said Alex was good at _____.

12 Write three more sentences. Then ask and answer.

Find someone who...
- can ride a horse.
- could swim when they were a baby.
- is good at climbing trees.
- could read when they were five years old.
- is good at drawing.
- can fish.
- is good at singing.
- _____.
- _____.
- _____.

Are you good at climbing trees?

Yes, I am!

Reading and Writing Part 6

1 Look and read and write.

Remember to write clearly
and check your answers carefully!

Examples

The girl next to the cage is wearing   _a blue dress_ .

What's the woman painting?   _The boy's face_ .

Complete the sentences.

1 The man who is carrying the drinks is wearing a _____ .

2 There are three white rabbits and one _____ .

Answer the questions.

3 What is the girl in the orange T-shirt doing? _____ .

4 How many glasses of juice are there?   _____ .

Now write two sentences about the picture.

5 _____ .

6 _____ .

Speaking Part 1

2 ◀)86 **Listen and find the differences.**

> Use pronouns *this* and *that* when you point to the people and things in the pictures.

3 ▶ **Now watch the video and talk about your answers.**

14 Let's have a picnic!

1 🔊87 **Listen. Look and point.**

2 🔊88 **Write the words. Listen and check.**

cheese • pasta • soup • milkshake • noodles
pancakes • sauce • vegetables • ~~sandwiches~~ • salad

Look & Learn

sandwich**es**
box**es**

1 sandwiches
2 _____
3 _____
4 _____
5 _____

6 _____
7 _____
8 _____
9 _____
10 _____

3 **Do you eat it hot or cold? Write the words from exercise 2.**
Then write three more hot and cold food or drinks.

Hot	Cold

4 Write the words. Which one is different?

	i l e m	l i m e
1	o c t n c o u	_ _ _ _ _ _ _
2	e l n p p a p e i	_ _ _ _ _ _ _ _ _
3	a r t o r c	_ _ _ _ _ _
4	i k i w	_ _ _ _
5	o a n m g	_ _ _ _ _
6	m e a l e w t r o n	_ _ _ _ _ _ _ _ _ _

5 Student A, read and complete the sentences below. Student B, look at page 127. Then listen to your partner.

tomato • outside • bowl • fruit • vegetables

1  You eat this from a _____. You can find _____ or meat in it.

2 It's a big _____. It's green on the _____ and red on the inside.

3  You often eat this with _____ sauce.

6 🔊89 Say the Sounds How many syllables have the words got? Write 1, 2, 3 or 4. Listen and check.

pasta • coconut • pancakes • sandwich • kiwi • milkshake • sauce • cheese
soup • mango • salad • vegetable • watermelon • pineapple • noodles • lime

7 Say & Play Ask and answer questions to find the food in your menu.

MENU 1	MENU 2	MENU 3	MENU 4
noodles	soup	pasta	chicken
salad	sandwich	meatballs	beans
milkshake	water	orange juice	milk
cake	pancakes	watermelon	apples
pineapple	coconut	chocolate	ice cream

Have you got any noodles?

Yes. Here you are. / Sorry, I haven't got any.

8 🔊90 **Listen and read.**

How much salad would you like?

A big bowl, please!

Yuck! It's got sauce!

Yes, it's tomato sauce! Here's some milkshake.

Yuck! I don't like carrot milkshake! Have we got any sandwiches?

Yes, we've got cheese and mango sandwiches! How many would you like?

Oh Tom, cheese and mango sandwiches? What a terrible picnic!

Zoe likes my picnic.

Look & Learn

How **much** milkshake would you like?
How **many** sandwiches would you like?

▶ How much? How many? p. 142

9 🔊91 **Read and circle. Listen and check.**

1 How **much** / (**many**) vegetables do we need?

2 There are **some** / **any** carrots and potatoes.

3 Have we got **some** / **any** peas?

4 Let's put **some** / **any** beans in them, too.

5 Are there **some** / **any** tomatoes?

6 Do you want to make **some** / **any** tomato sauce?

7 How **much** / **many** ice cream have we got?

10 🔊91 **Which picture is Jane's kitchen? Listen again and tick (✔).**
Then answer the questions and write.

A

B

Are there any vegetables in Jane's kitchen?

Yes, there are. There are carrots, peas, tomatoes, onions and potatoes.

1 How many tomatoes are there? There are _____.

2 Is there any meat? _____.

3 How much ice cream is there? _____.

4 Are there any beans? _____.

5 There _____.

6 There _____.

11 **Say & Play Choose a picture. Then ask and answer questions.**

A

B

C

D

Is there any fruit?

Yes, there are some mangoes.

How many mangoes are there?

Three.

Reading and Writing Part 5

1 **Look at the pictures and read the story. Write some words to complete the sentences about the story. You can use 1, 2 or 3 words.**

> Think about the sentences. Read them carefully. Remember to write words like *a* and *the*.

THE BEST COOK

Pat is eleven years old and he loves cooking. On Saturdays he makes pancakes for breakfast and sandwiches for lunch. Sometimes he cooks pasta or noodles for dinner. Everyone loves his food. One day Pat's sister saw a poster at school. It said: 'Do you like cooking? Are you between 10 and 14 years old? *Best Cook* needs young cooks!' Pat's sister sent a video of Pat to *Best Cook*.

Examples

Pat enjoys __cooking__.

Pat _makes pancakes_ for breakfast on Saturdays.

Questions

1 Pat's family enjoys eating the _____ Pat makes.

2 Pat's sister made _____ of Pat for *Best Cook*.

One day Pat got an email. 'Well done! We would like to invite you to be on *Best Cook*.' Pat was very surprised but he was happy, too. On the big day, Pat was a little frightened because all the other children were older than him. 'I don't know what to cook!' he said. Pat saw the food on the table: chicken, rice, onions, peas and cheese. Then he had an idea and he started cooking.

3 Pat was surprised when he read _____.

4 The other children were _____ than Pat.

5 At first, Pat didn't _____ what food to cook.

When the children finished cooking, a man and a woman ate some of the food. 'Your rice is fantastic!' the woman said to Pat. 'You're the best cook!' the man said. They gave Pat a beautiful cup. 'This cup is for you, Grandma!' Pat said. 'Thank you for teaching me to cook your favourite rice!'

6 The man told Pat he was _____.

7 Pat gave the cup to his _____.

Speaking Part 3

2 🔊92 **Listen and say which one is different.**

3 ▶ **Now watch the video and talk about your answers.**

15 Let's play!

1 🔊93 **Listen. Look and point.**

2 🔊94 **Write the numbers.**
Listen and check.

comic	3	rug		
blanket		net		
camera		rubber		
model		crayon		
ruler		lamp		

3 🔊95 **Tick (✔) the toys which are in the picture. Listen and check.**

kite		truck	
skateboard		plane	
bike		teddy	
board game		robot	
boat		football	
doll		monster	
train		helicopter	

4 Where does Lucy put her things? Look and write *in* or *on*.

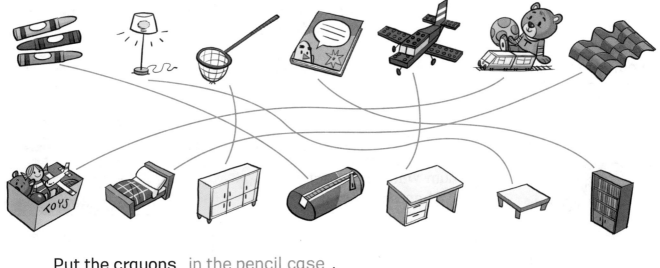

Put the crayons _in the pencil case_ .

1 Put the lamp _____ .
2 Put the net _____ .
3 Put the comic _____ .
4 Put the model _____ .
5 Put the toys _____ .
6 Put the blanket _____ .

5 🔊96 Listen and write *Alice*, *Eva*, *Paul* or *Bill*.

_____

_____

_____

_____

6 Say & Play Colour and put the things in the bedroom. Then tell your partner.

Put the comic (on the desk).
Colour it red.

OK.

7 🔊97 **Listen and read.**

Hi, Lucy. Shall I help you clean your room?

Yes, please! Mum was very angry when she saw it!

Can you put those clothes on the desk?

On the desk? How about in the cupboard?

Oh, no! Lucy!

Sorry, Charlie. Let's pick them up.

Later...

Your room looks better now. What about my room?

Oh, Charlie!

Look & Learn

Shall I help you?
How/What about my room?

8 **Read and complete.**

How • about (x 2) • Shall • what

Sam I don't know what toy to take to school tomorrow.

Ben Shall I help you choose? Don't take your football. We have to play in the classroom, not outside.

Sam OK. **(1)** _____ about my kite?

Ben You can't fly a kite in the classroom!

Sam All right. What **(2)** _____ my favourite teddy bear?

Ben That's better. But **(3)** _____ about something that more children can play with?

Sam How **(4)** _____ my model? It's a boat.

Ben I know! How about taking this board game? Everyone likes playing this!

Sam What a great idea!

Tomorrow it's 'Play Day'. Take a toy to school and play with it. Which toy do you want to take?

9 **Write sentences. Then ask and answer.**

to the shop? / Shall / go / I
Shall I go to the shop?

I / help you / those bags? / carry / Shall

10 **Read and colour the squares.**

It's a beautiful day today!	It rained yesterday.	How about eating at a café?	Sorry, I don't like cheese.
Yes, it is. How about a walk in the countryside?	Great idea! Shall I bring a picnic?	Yes, please. I've got some fruit.	That's OK.
No, thanks. I'm not hungry.	No, let's take juice. How about going by bike?	What about drinks? Shall I bring water?	You must drink 5 glasses of water every day.
Would you like some milkshake?	No, I hurt my arm yesterday. Let's go by bus.	OK. What about the 10 o'clock bus?	Fantastic! See you then.

11 **Say & Play** **What do you want to do on Saturday? Talk in groups.**

Let's... ?
How/What about... ?

That's a good idea.
What a great idea!
OK, that's fun.
Sorry, I don't like...

How about going to the shopping centre?

Sorry, I don't like shopping. What about the park?

Listening Part 1

1 🔊98 **Listen and draw lines. There is one example.**

Mark   Sue   Alex   Daisy

Listen for the answers to these questions about the people in the picture: What do they look like? What are they doing? What are they wearing or carrying?

Sally   Nick   Paul

Reading and Writing Part 3

2 **Read the story. Choose a word from the box.
Write the correct word next to numbers 1-5.
There is one example.**

Think about what the words mean. Are they nouns, verbs or adjectives?

Dan loves making things. Last Monday, Dan's teacher told the class to make a model of a room in a house. 'You can work with a friend', she said. 'Choose a room and think about what's inside it. Then think about what _shape_ these things are: are they circles or squares?' 'This is great!' said Dan.

Dan and Sam had lots of (1) _____ but they didn't know which one to choose. 'What about a bathroom?' Sam said. 'I don't know how to make a shower' said Dan. 'It's too (2) _____. How about a bedroom?' 'That's a great idea!' said Sam. First, they made the room from an old (3) _____.

'Let's (4) _____ a bed and a cupboard.' The other children worked quickly but Dan and Sam worked slowly. After lunch, the teacher looked at all the models. She loved their bedroom. 'Well done, Dan and Sam!' said the teacher. 'Your model is (5) _____!'

Example shape	build	ideas
climb	box	wrong
brilliant	dream	difficult

(6) **Now choose the best name for the story. Tick one box.**

Dan's bedroom. ☐   A fun lesson. ☐   Sam and Dan make a box. ☐

16 On the Internet

1 🔊99 Listen. Look and point.

2 🔊99 Write the words. Listen again and check.

> websites • e-books • apps • texts • keyboard • ~~laptop~~ • video • emails

Tom does homework on his _laptop_ .

1 Tom looks at _____ on the Internet.
2 Tom writes with the _____ .
3 Tom's grandmother sends _____ .
4 Tom's got lots of _____ on his tablet.
5 Tom is watching a _____ about cats.
6 Tom sends _____ to his friends.
7 Tom often reads _____ .

3 Read and circle the nouns in green and the verbs in blue.

a I sent my mum a (text.)
b (Text) me when you get there.

1 a I'm sending him an email about the party.
b Can you email the teacher, please?

2 a I sometimes video Lucy when she's dancing!
b I'm watching a funny video.

Look & Learn

Text, email and **video** can be nouns or verbs!

4 Read and complete.

Q Search

Be safe on the Internet

* Don't tell anyone your 21 KING STREET <u>address</u> or your phone number.

* Only answer **(1)** _____ or emails from people you know.

* Don't send **(2)** _____ to people you don't know.

* Tell a grown-up if an **(3)** _____ or website makes you sad or afraid.

* Only watch videos on **(4)** _____ that are safe for children.

* Ask a grown-up before you get a new **(5)** _____ .

5 ◀)100 Read and write. Listen and check.

film • band • DVD • ~~music~~ • videos • CDs

I love listening to ___music___ . My favourite **(1)** _____ is called Orange Kiwi. I've got all their **(2)** _____ . I like watching **(3)** _____ of their songs. They're fantastic dancers!

Saturday evening is like a cinema in my house. Sometimes we watch a new **(4)** _____ on the Internet. But I like watching old movies on **(5)** _____ , too.

6 Answer the questions. Then ask and answer with your partner.

1 Have you got the **Internet** in your classroom?
2 Which **websites** do you and your family look at?
3 Do you do homework on a **computer** or **laptop**?
4 Do you like writing with a **keyboard** or with a pen?
5 Do you read **e-books**?
6 What are your favourite **apps**?
7 Do you listen to **CDs** or watch **DVDs**? Which ones?
8 Who's your favourite **band** or singer?

7 🔊101 **Listen and read.**

▶ *who, which, where* p. 143

8 **Read and write *who*, *which* or *where*.**

The video _which_ the boys are watching is very boring.

1 The girl _____ is reading about robots is wearing purple trousers.

2 The table _____ the old man is sitting is brown.

3 The bookcase _____ has got children's books is blue.

4 The woman _____ is giving the boy an e-book has got blonde hair.

5 The book _____ the older girl is reading is a comic.

9 **Read the sentences in exercise 8 again. Say *yes* or *no*.**

> The video which the boys are watching is very boring.

> No, it isn't! The video which the boys are watching is very funny!

10 **Say & Play Student A, colour and draw circles on the picture. Student B, look at page 128. Tell your partner.**

The girl who is watching a movie has a (green) jacket.

11 **Look at the picture again. Ask and answer the questions with *I think...***

1. What is the e-book which the woman is reading about?
2. What's in the woman's bag?
3. What do people buy in this shop?
4. Is the video which the boy is watching a music video or a film?
5. What does the message which the man is sending say?

I think the e-book is about (a family).

105

MOVERS PRACTICE

Listening Part 4

1 🔊 **102 Listen and tick (✔) the box.**
There is one example.

Read the question first.
Listen to the end,
then write your answer.

What is the DVD about?

A  B  ✔ C

1 What is on television this evening?

A  B  C

2 Who does Eva have to send a text message to?

A  B  C

3 What is the e-book about?

A  B 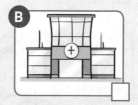 C

4 What is Hugo doing on his laptop?

A  B  C

5 Which CD is Julia's favourite?

A  B  C

Speaking Part 2

2 🔊 **103** **Listen and tell the story.**

SAM BUYS A CAMERA

> Tell the story with different words, e.g. *have got, can / can't, have to / must.*

Sam

TECH SHOP

3 ▶ **Now watch the** video **and talk about your answers.**

1 **Read and write.**

①

What am I?

I come to your town every year.
Children love me, they have lots of
fun here. Go into the circus then come
outside. Sail a boat, ride a horse and go
on my rides. I'm a _____.

②

What am I?

Open me and watch a video.
Send an email to all the people you
know. Go on the Internet, look at
a website. Put your fingers on my
keyboard to write. I'm a _____.

③

What am I?

I am all the colours in the rainbow.
A garden or a farm is where I grow.
'Eat five a day!' doctors always say.
Try to eat me every day.
I'm a _____.

④

What am I?

I'm not a toy but I live on your bed.
I can be any colour: brown, green or red.
At a picnic you sit on me when you eat.
When it's cold put me on your shoulders,
legs and feet! I'm a _____.

2 **Make words. Then complete the text.**

ha	tened
ea	erous
dang	ppy
hun	gry
sal	ave
br	ad
frigh	sy

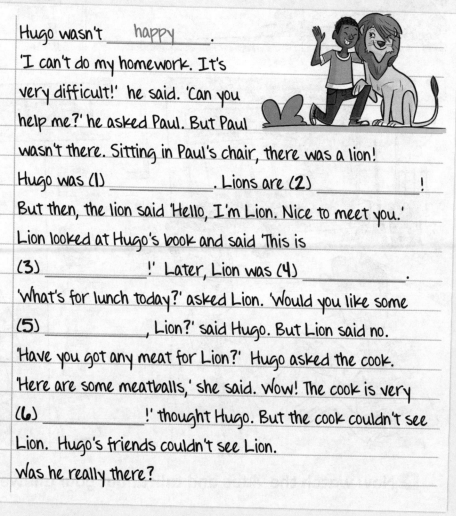

Hugo wasn't ___happy___.
'I can't do my homework. It's
very difficult!' he said. 'Can you
help me?' he asked Paul. But Paul
wasn't there. Sitting in Paul's chair, there was a lion!
Hugo was (1) _____. Lions are (2) _____!
But then, the lion said 'Hello, I'm Lion. Nice to meet you.'
Lion looked at Hugo's book and said 'This is
(3) _____!' Later, Lion was (4) _____.
'What's for lunch today?' asked Lion. 'Would you like some
(5) _____, Lion?' said Hugo. But Lion said no.
'Have you got any meat for Lion?' Hugo asked the cook.
'Here are some meatballs,' she said. Wow! The cook is very
(6) _____!' thought Hugo. But the cook couldn't see
Lion. Hugo's friends couldn't see Lion.
Was he really there?

3 ▶ **Watch the video. Then complete. You don't need all the words.**

> can • could • can't • couldn't
> some • any • much • many
> shall • which • who

At the funfair

1 How _____ sandwiches did you eat?

2 There isn't _____ orange juice.

3 'Could he ride a horse when he was six?'
'No, he _____.'

4 She's the girl _____ I saw in the video.

5 Can I read the comic _____ you bought yesterday?

4 **Say & Play** Find eight differences. Talk to your partner about the pictures.

MOVERS PRACTICE TEST

Listening Part 1

🔊 104 **Listen and draw lines. There is one example.**

Daisy Sam Bill Jim

Fred Eva Jack

Listening Part 2

🔊 **105** **Listen and write. There is one example.**

A FUN DAY

Where the park is:	next to	_the lake_
1 Name of the park:	_____ Water Park	
2 Bus number:	_____	
3 Things people do:	swimming and _____	
4 What to wear:	_____	
5 Food people buy:	_____ and salad	

Listening Part 3

🔊 106 **Mr Rivers is telling Julia about the people in his family and their favourite animals. Which is each person's favourite animal?**

Listen and write a letter in each box. There is one example.

his son	F
his aunt	
his cousin	
his father	
his sister	
his daughter	

A

B

C

D

E

F

G

H

Listening Part 4

🔊 107 **Listen and tick (✔) the box. There is one example.**

Where is the toothpaste?

A  ✔

B

C

1 What is Jack's mum having for dinner?

A

B

C

2 What was the matter with Vicky yesterday?

A

B

C

3 Who is Jane's uncle?

A

B

C

4 What does Sally want to be?

A

B

C

5 Which picture did Bill take?

A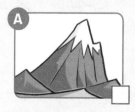

B

C

Listening Part 5

🔊 108 **Listen and colour and write. There is one example.**

Reading and Writing Part 1

Look and read. Choose the correct words and write them on the lines.
There is one example.

a city

ice

a nurse

a shopping centre

a dentist

snow

coffee

a bowl

Example

This is cold and white and it falls from the sky. ___snow___

Questions

1 Grown-ups often drink this with their breakfast. _____

2 You go to see this person when you have got toothache. _____

3 Lots of people live and work in this place. _____

4 You buy all kinds of things here. _____

5 You eat food like soup or ice cream in this. _____

Reading and Writing Part 2

Read the text and choose the best answer.

Example

Anna   Hi, Paul. You don't look well. Are you OK?

Paul   A Very well, thank you.
       B No, I feel ill.
       C Yes, it's fine.

Questions

1 Anna What's the matter?

Paul   A Are you sick?
       B Today is Wednesday.
       C I've got a headache.

2 Anna Shall I get you a glass of water?

Paul   A Yes, please.
       B Yes, so do I.
       C I want it.

3 Anna You must go to bed, now.

Paul   A You're asleep.
       B But I'm not tired!
       C Did you brush your teeth?

4 Anna OK, but don't watch TV. It makes your headache worse.

Paul   A Yes, you're right.
       B No, I don't.
       C What's on TV?

5 Anna Let's go to the park when you're better.

Paul   A I'm going to the park.
       B What a nice idea!
       C Can you take my dog for a walk?

6 Paul I'm feeling much better now!

Anna   A It's terrible!
       B Let's call the doctor.
       C That's great!

Reading and Writing Part 3

Read the story. Choose a word from the box. Write the correct word next to numbers 1-5. There is one example.

Peter enjoys being outside and doing sports. Last weekend, his parents took him to a school in the _forest_ . There were lots of children doing different sports. 'Goodbye, Peter! See you on Sunday,' Peter's mum said.

A teacher showed Peter his **(1)** _____ and where to put his bag. Then they went outside and Peter saw some children **(2)** _____ in the river. Peter put his net in the water for a long time but he didn't catch a fish.

In the afternoon, the children played football. Peter ran quickly and **(3)** _____ the ball into the net. He scored three goals and everyone was very happy. That evening, they all watched a **(4)** _____ . Peter was very tired and at eight o'clock he was **(5)** _____!

Example forest	CD	asleep
kicked	fishing	movie
hopping	thirsty	bedroom

(6) Now choose the best name for the story. Tick one box.

A fun weekend ☐   The best player ☐   Peter's favourite sport ☐

Reading and Writing Part 4

Read the text. Choose the right words and write them on the lines.

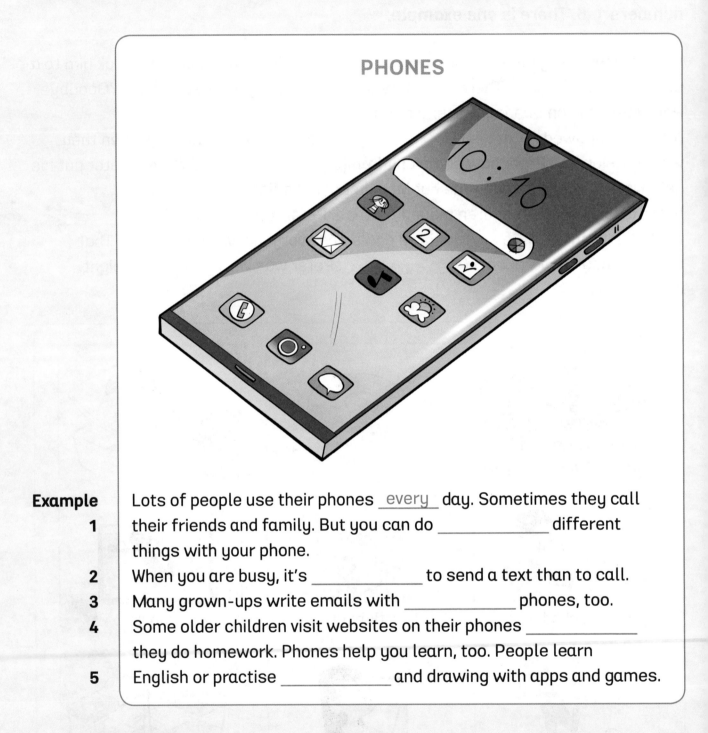

PHONES

Example	Lots of people use their phones _every_ day. Sometimes they call
1	their friends and family. But you can do _____ different things with your phone.
2	When you are busy, it's _____ to send a text than to call.
3	Many grown-ups write emails with _____ phones, too.
4	Some older children visit websites on their phones _____ they do homework. Phones help you learn, too. People learn
5	English or practise _____ and drawing with apps and games.

Example	some	every	any
1	a lot of	much	most
2	easiest	easy	easier
3	their	they	your
4	what	when	because
5	reading	read	reads

Reading and Writing Part 5

Look at the pictures and read the story. Write some words to complete the sentences about the story. You can use 1, 2 or 3 words.

A DAY IN THE CITY

Lily lived with her parents and older brother in a small town. On Saturdays, Lily's grandparents sometimes took Lily and her brother Hugo to visit a new place. Last Saturday, they all went to see Lily's uncle at his new flat in the city. They caught the bus at the bus stop near the park. Lily's grandmother gave the children some orange juice to drink on the bus.

Examples

Lily's home was in _a small town_ .

Lily and Hugo sometimes went out with their _grandparents_ .

Questions

1 Lily and Hugo took the bus to the _____ with their grandparents.

2 On the bus, they had a drink of _____ .

'Look, we're at the bus station!' said Lily. 'It's huge!' The bus station was new and it had shops and a café inside. Grandpa pointed to his map. 'Here's Uncle Jim's flat,' he said. They walked along a street with cafés and they came to a large square. 'A market!' said Lily. 'Can I buy Uncle Jim a present? Please!' 'That's a nice idea!' said Grandpa.

3 There were some _____ in the bus station.

4 Grandpa looked at the map and found Uncle Jim's _____ .

5 Lucy wanted to _____ for her uncle at the market.

'There's the library,' said Hugo. 'Uncle Jim lives opposite the library.' They saw Uncle Jim, waving from his balcony. They went upstairs and Lily gave Uncle Jim a plant from the market.

'This is for your new flat,' she said. 'Thank you!' said Uncle Jim. 'It's very pretty.'

'Now let's see the city,' he said. They walked around and looked at the famous buildings. Then they had lunch in a café.

Then, Lily, Hugo and their grandparents got on the bus and went home.

6 Lily's uncle thought the plant was _____.

7 The family saw some _____ in the city before lunch.

Reading and Writing Part 6

Look and read and write.

Examples

The baby sitting under the tree is ___crying___ .

What's the grandfather fixing? ___The boy's bike___ .

Complete the sentences.

1   The woman with the hat is working on her _____ .

2   The kittens are playing with _____ .

Answer the questions.

3   What's the grandmother doing? _____ .

4   Where is the dog? _____ .

Now write two sentences about the picture.

5   _____ .

6   _____ .

MOVERS PRACTICE TEST

Speaking Part 1

🔊 109 **Listen and find the differences.**

Speaking Part 2

🔊 110 **Listen and tell the story.**

JIM TAKES BOUNCER FOR A WALK

Jim

MOVERS PRACTICE TEST

Speaking Part 3

🔊 111 **Listen and say which one is different.**

Speaking Part 4

🔊 112 **Listen and answer the questions.**

Speaking cards

▶ Unit 4 • page 27, exercise 11

▶ Unit 5 • page 33, exercise 7

▶ Unit 5 • page 35, exercise 11

	Monday	Tuesday	Wednesday	Thursday	Friday	Saturday	Sunday

Speaking cards

▶ Unit 8 • page 51, exercise 6

Student B

Instructions for Student A

Draw two **plants** on the beach.

Draw three **shells** on the sand in front of the house.

Draw some **leaves** on the tree and colour them green.

Draw some **rocks** at the bottom of the sea.

▶ Unit 12 • page 77, exercise 6

Speaking cards

▶ Unit 12 • page 79, exercise 11

	go to bed	drink water	put on a hat	put ice on	put a hot towel on

(boy)	X	✔	X	X	✔
(girl)					
(man)	✔	✔	✔	X	✔

▶ Unit 14 • page 91, exercise 5

> fruit • lemon • milk • bread • yellow

1  You make this cold drink with _____ and fruit.

2 This is _____ and you can eat it between _____.

3 It's a small green _____. It's like a _____.

Speaking cards

▶ Unit 16 • page 105, exercise 10

Wordlist

0 · Hello!
Numbers

one _____

two _____

three _____

four _____

five _____

six _____

seven _____

eight _____

nine _____

ten _____

eleven _____

twelve _____

thirteen _____

twenty _____

twenty-one _____

twenty-two _____

thirty _____

forty _____

fifty _____

sixty _____

seventy _____

eighty _____

ninety _____

one hundred _____

first _____

second _____

third _____

fourth _____

fifth _____

sixth _____

seventh _____

eighth _____

ninth _____

tenth _____

eleventh _____

twelfth _____

thirteenth _____

twentieth _____

Questions & Expressions

What's your name? _____

How old are you? _____

Who's that? _____

How do you spell it? _____

1 · My family
Family & friends

aunt _____

brother _____

cousin _____

daughter _____

father _____

grandchildren _____

granddaughter _____

grandfather _____

grandmother _____

grandparent _____

grandson _____

Wordlist

grown-up _____

mother _____

parent _____

sister _____

son _____

uncle _____

Describing people

beard _____

curly _____

fair _____

fat _____

glasses _____

long _____

moustache _____

short _____

straight _____

tall _____

thin _____

2 · My week

Days of the week

Monday _____

Tuesday _____

Wednesday _____

Thursday _____

Friday _____

Saturday _____

Sunday _____

Adverbs and expressions of frequency

always _____

every day _____

never _____

often _____

sometimes _____

at the weekend _____

After-school activities

do homework _____

draw pictures _____

go swimming _____

go to basketball practice _____

go to somebody's house _____

go to the park _____

have a piano lesson _____

have my English lesson _____

learn the guitar _____

play computer games _____

ride my bike _____

read books _____

take photos _____

watch TV _____

3 At home

The home (1)

address _____

armchair _____

balcony _____

Wordlist

basement _____

bath _____

bed _____

bookcase _____

clock _____

computer _____

cupboard _____

desk _____

downstairs _____

floor _____

lamp _____

lift / elevator _____

mirror _____

plant _____

roof _____

rug _____

shower _____

sofa _____

stairs _____

toothbrush _____

toothpaste _____

towel _____

upstairs _____

Home activities

clean _____

dry yourself _____

cook _____

enjoy _____

fix _____

get dressed _____

go to bed _____

have a shower _____

have dinner _____

help _____

make (a cake) _____

phone _____

put on _____

sit _____

sleep _____

smile _____

take off _____

wake up _____

wash _____

work _____

4 · My city

Places

bus station _____

café _____

car park _____

cinema _____

hospital _____

library _____

market _____

shopping centre / center _____

sports centre / center _____

square _____

station _____

swimming pool _____

Wordlist

Transport

bike _____

boat _____

bus _____

bus stop _____

car _____

catch _____

drive _____

driver _____

fly _____

helicopter _____

lorry / truck _____

plane _____

road _____

station _____

ticket _____

train _____

Prepositions of place

above _____

behind _____

below _____

between _____

in front of _____

near _____

next to _____

opposite _____

5 · It's a sunny day
Weather

cloud _____

cloudy _____

dry _____

hot _____

ice _____

rain _____

rainbow _____

sky _____

snow _____

sun _____

sunny _____

weather _____

wet _____

wind _____

windy _____

Questions & Expressions

What's the weather like? _____

It's (sunny). _____

There's (the sun). _____

6 · A shopping day
Clothes

bag _____

baseball cap _____

boots _____

coat _____

dress _____

Wordlist

handbag _____

hat _____

helmet _____

jacket _____

jeans _____

scarf _____

shirt _____

shoe _____

skirt _____

socks _____

sweater _____

swimsuit _____

trousers _____

T-shirt _____

Questions & Expressions

What are you wearing? _____

I'm wearing (a T-shirt). _____

7 · Lucy's birthday party

Work

clown _____

cook _____

dentist _____

doctor _____

driver _____

farmer _____

film star / movie star _____

nurse _____

pirate _____

pop star _____

Food & drinks • Containers

bottle _____

bowl _____

box _____

cup _____

glass _____

plate _____

Food & drinks (1)

beans _____

chicken _____

chips _____

coffee _____

egg _____

fish _____

grapes _____

hot chocolate _____

ice cream _____

juice _____

lemonade _____

meat _____

meatballs _____

milk _____

rice _____

sausage _____

tea _____

water _____

Wordlist

8 · Our beautiful world
The world around us

beach _____

field _____

forest _____

grass _____

island _____

lake _____

leaf _____

mountain _____

plant _____

river _____

road _____

rock _____

sand _____

sea _____

shell _____

tree _____

village _____

waterfall _____

wave _____

Expressions

go for a drive _____

go for an ice cream _____

go for a bike ride _____

go for a walk _____

go for a swim _____

9 · At the farm
Animals (1)

bee _____

bird _____

cage _____

cat _____

chicken _____

cow _____

dog _____

donkey _____

duck _____

fly _____

frog _____

goat _____

horse _____

kitten _____

parrot _____

puppy _____

rabbit _____

sheep _____

Adjectives

asleep _____

awake _____

big _____

clever _____

good _____

huge _____

hungry _____

naughty _____

Wordlist

pretty _____

silly _____

small _____

strong _____

thirsty _____

ugly _____

weak _____

10 · The animal park
Animals (2)

bat _____

bear _____

crocodile _____

dolphin _____

elephant _____

fish _____

giraffe _____

hippo _____

kangaroo _____

lion _____

monkey _____

panda _____

penguin _____

polar bear _____

shark _____

snail _____

snake _____

spider _____

tiger _____

whale _____

zebra _____

Adjectives & adverbs

beautiful _____

carefully _____

dangerous _____

hungry _____

loud _____

quickly _____

quietly _____

slowly _____

surprised _____

terrible _____

well _____

wet _____

11 · At the sports centre
Sports & leisure (1)

badminton _____

baseball _____

basketball _____

bounce _____

climb _____

football / soccer _____

hit _____

hockey _____

hop _____

ice skates _____

ice skating _____

jump _____

Wordlist

kick _____

net _____

player _____

racket _____

roller skates _____

roller skating _____

run _____

score _____

skate _____

skateboard _____

skateboarding _____

skip _____

table tennis _____

tennis _____

back _____

ear _____

eye _____

foot _____

hand _____

head _____

leg _____

mouth _____

neck _____

nose _____

shoulder _____

stomach _____

tooth _____

12 · I'm not well

Health

cold _____

cough _____

earache _____

fine _____

headache _____

hurt _____

ill _____

stomach-ache _____

temperature _____

toothache _____

The body and the face

arm _____

Questions

What's the matter? _____

13 · At the funfair

Sports & leisure (2)

catch _____

drop _____

fall _____

fish _____

ride _____

sail _____

throw _____

wave _____

Adjectives

brave _____

Wordlist

dangerous _____

difficult _____

easy _____

frightened _____

safe _____

Expressions

I'm good at (tennis). _____

14 · Let's have a picnic!
Food & drinks (2)

apple _____

beans _____

cake _____

carrot _____

cheese _____

chicken _____

chocolate _____

coconut _____

fruit _____

kiwi _____

lime _____

mango _____

milk _____

milkshake _____

noodles _____

orange juice _____

pancake _____

pasta _____

pineapple _____

salad _____

sandwich _____

sauce _____

sausage _____

soup _____

tomato _____

vegetable _____

water _____

watermelon _____

Questions & Expressions

Have you got any (milkshake)? _____

Yes. Here you are. _____

Sorry. I haven't got any. _____

How much (water)? _____

How many (carrots)? _____

15 · Let's play!
The home (2)

bike _____

blanket _____

board game _____

boat _____

bookcase _____

camera _____

comic _____

crayon _____

cupboard _____

desk _____

doll _____

Wordlist

football _____

helicopter _____

kite _____

lamp _____

model _____

monster _____

net _____

plane _____

robot _____

rubber _____

rug _____

ruler _____

skateboard _____

teddy _____

train _____

truck _____

film / movie _____

internet _____

keyboard _____

laptop _____

music _____

text _____

video _____

website _____

Expressions

I think (she's happy). _____

Questions

Shall I (help you)? _____

What about (my room)? _____

How about (going to the park)? _____

16 · On the Internet

Sports & leisure (3)

app _____

band _____

CD _____

DVD _____

e-book _____

email _____

Grammar tables

be

AFFIRMATIVE FORM	NEGATIVE FORM	INTERROGATIVE FORM	SHORT ANSWERS
I'm Lucy.	I'm not Lucy.	Am I Lucy?	Yes, I am.
			No, I'm not.
You're Tom.	You aren't Tom.	Are you Tom?	Yes, you are.
			No, you aren't.
He's Tom.	He isn't Tom.	Is he Tom?	Yes, he is.
			No, he isn't.
She's Lucy.	She's not Lucy.	Is she Lucy?	Yes, she is.
			No, she isn't.
It's a book.	It isn't a book.	Is it a book?	Yes, it is.
			No, it isn't.
We're Lucy and Tom.	We aren't Lucy and Tom.	Are we Lucy and Tom?	Yes, we are.
			No, we aren't.
You're Lucy and Tom.	You aren't Lucy and Tom.	Are you Lucy and Tom?	Yes, you are.
			No, you aren't.
They're Lucy and Tom.	They aren't Lucy and Tom.	Are they Lucy and Tom?	Yes, they are.
			No, they aren't.

have got

AFFIRMATIVE FORM	NEGATIVE FORM	INTERROGATIVE FORM	SHORT ANSWERS
I've got fair hair.	I haven't got fair hair.	Have I got fair hair?	Yes, I have.
			No, I haven't.
You've got fair hair.	You haven't got fair hair.	Have you got fair hair?	Yes, you have.
			No, you haven't.
He's got blue eyes.	He hasn't got blue eyes.	Has he got blue eyes?	Yes, he has.
			No, he hasn't.
She's got blue eyes.	She hasn't got blue eyes.	Has she got blue eyes?	Yes, she has.
			No, she hasn't.
It's got a long tail.	It hasn't got a long tail.	Has it got a long tail?	Yes, it has.
			No, it hasn't.
We've got long legs.	We haven't got long legs.	Have we got long legs?	Yes, we have.
			No, we haven't.
You've got long legs.	You haven't got long legs.	Have you got long legs?	Yes, you have.
			No, you haven't.
They've got long legs.	They haven't got long legs.	Have they got long legs?	Yes, they have.
			No, they haven't.

Grammar tables

Present simple

AFFIRMATIVE FORM	NEGATIVE FORM	INTERROGATIVE FORM	SHORT ANSWERS
I / You jump.	I / You **don't** jump.	**Do** I / you jump?	Yes, I / you **do**.
			No, I / you **don't**.
He / She / It jumps.	He / She / It **doesn't** jump.	**Does** he / she / it jump?	Yes, he / she / it **does**.
			No, he / she / it **doesn't**.
We / You / They jump.	We / You / They **don't** jump.	**Do** we / you / they jump?	Yes, we / you / they **do**.
			No, we / you / they **don't**.

Present continuous

AFFIRMATIVE FORM	NEGATIVE FORM	INTERROGATIVE FORM	SHORT ANSWERS
I'm playing.	I'm **not** playing.	**Am** I playing?	Yes, I **am**.
			No, I'm **not**.
You're playing.	You **aren't** playing.	**Are** you playing?	Yes, you **are**.
			No, you **aren't**.
He / She / It's playing.	He / She / It **isn't** playing.	**Is** he / she / it playing?	Yes, he / she / it **is**.
			No, he / she / it **isn't**.
We're playing.	We **aren't** playing.	**Are** we playing?	Yes, we **are**.
			No, we **aren't**.
You're playing.	You **aren't** playing.	**Are** you playing?	Yes, you **are**.
			No, you **aren't**.
They're playing.	They **aren't** playing.	**Are** they playing?	Yes, they **are**.
			No, they **aren't**.

there is / there are

AFFIRMATIVE FORM	NEGATIVE FORM	INTERROGATIVE FORM	SHORT ANSWERS
There's a bed.	**There isn't** a bed.	**Is there** a bed?	Yes, **there is**.
			No, **there isn't**.
There are two windows.	**There aren't** two windows.	**Are there** two windows?	Yes, **there are**.
			No, **there aren't**.

Grammar tables

was / were

AFFIRMATIVE FORM	NEGATIVE FORM	INTERROGATIVE FORM	SHORT ANSWERS
I **was** hungry.	I **wasn't** hungry.	**Was** I hungry?	Yes, I **was**.
			No, I **wasn't**.
You **were** hungry.	You **weren't** hungry.	**Were** you hungry?	Yes, you **were**.
			No, you **weren't**.
He **was** hungry.	He **wasn't** hungry.	**Was** he hungry?	Yes, he **was**.
			No, he **wasn't**.
She **was** hungry.	She **wasn't** hungry.	**Was** she hungry?	Yes, she **was**.
			No, she **wasn't**.
It **was** hungry.	It **wasn't** hungry.	**Was** it hungry?	Yes, it **was**.
			No, it **wasn't**.
We **were** hungry.	We **weren't** hungry.	**Were** we hungry?	Yes, we **were**.
			No, we **weren't**.
You **were** hungry.	You **weren't** hungry.	**Were** you hungry?	Yes, you **were**.
			No, you **weren't**.
They **were** hungry.	They **weren't** hungry.	**Were** they hungry?	Yes, they **were**.
			No, they **weren't**.

Past simple

AFFIRMATIVE FORM	NEGATIVE FORM	INTERROGATIVE FORM	SHORT ANSWERS
I / you jump**ed**.	I / you **didn't** jump.	**Did** I / you jump?	Yes, I / you **did**.
			No, I / you **didn't**.
He / She / It jump**ed**.	He / She / It **didn't** jump.	**Did** he / she / it jump?	Yes, he / she / it **did**.
			No, he / she / it **didn't**.
We / You / They jump**ed**.	We / You / They **didn't** jump.	**Did** we / you / they jump?	Yes, we / you / they **did**.
			No, we / you / they **didn't**.

Comparatives & Superlatives

	ADJECTIVES	COMPARATIVE ADJECTIVES	SUPERLATIVE ADJECTIVES
Short adjectives	strong	**stronger than** *Horses are **stronger than** parrots.*	**the strongest** *Horses are **the strongest** animals on the farm.*
Long adjectives	dangerous	**more dangerous than** *Lions are **more dangerous than** crocodiles.*	**the most dangerous** *Lions are **the most dangerous** animals in the world.*
Irregular adjectives	good	**better than** *Penguins are **better** parents **than** crocodiles.*	**the best** *Penguins are **the best** parents.*
	bad	**worse than** *Snakes are **worse** pets **than** parrots.*	**the worst** *Snakes are **the worst** pets.*

141

Grammar tables

must

AFFIRMATIVE FORM	NEGATIVE FORM	INTERROGATIVE FORM	SHORT ANSWERS
I / You / He / She / It / We / You / They **must** bounce the ball.	I / You / He / She / It / We / You / They **mustn't** bounce the ball.	**Must** I / you / he / she / it / we / you / they bounce the ball?	Yes, I / you / he / she / it / we / you / they **must**.
			No, I / you / he / she / it / we / you / they **mustn't**.

have to

AFFIRMATIVE FORM	NEGATIVE FORM	INTERROGATIVE FORM	SHORT ANSWERS
I / you **have to** sleep.	I / you **don't have to** sleep.	**Do** I / you **have to** sleep?	Yes, I / you **do**.
			No, I / you **don't**.
He / She / It **has to** sleep.	He / She / It **doesn't have to** sleep.	**Does** he / she / it **have to** sleep?	Yes, he / she / it **does**.
			No, he / she / it **doesn't**.
We / You / They **have to** sleep.	We / You / They **don't have to** sleep.	**Do** we / you / they **have to** sleep?	Yes, we / you / they **do**.
			No, we / you / they **don't**.

could

AFFIRMATIVE FORM	NEGATIVE FORM	INTERROGATIVE FORM	SHORT ANSWERS
I / You / He / She / It / We / You / They **could** skate.	I / You / He / She / It / We / You / They **couldn't** skate.	**Could** I / you / he / she / it / we / you / they skate?	Yes, I / you / he / she / it / we / you / they **could**.
			No, I / you / he / she / it / we / you / they **couldn't**.

some, any

		AFFIRMATIVE SENTENCE	NEGATIVE SENTENCE	INTERROGATIVE SENTENCE
Countable nouns	one	I've got **a** sandwich.	I haven't got **a** sandwich.	Have you got **a** sandwich?
	more than one	I've got **some** sandwiches.	I haven't got **any** sandwiches.	Have you got **any** sandwiches?
Uncountable nouns		I've got **some** milkshake.	I haven't got **any** milkshake.	Have you got **any** milkshake?

How many, How much

	INTERROGATIVE SENTENCE
Countable nouns	**How many** sandwiches have you got?
Uncountable nouns	**How much** milkshake have you got?

Grammar tables

who / which / where

people	who	Ben is the boy **who** came to the countryside with me.
things	which	The video **which** the boys are watching is very boring.
places	where	Is that **where** you swam in the river?

Irregular verbs

INFINITIVE	PAST SIMPLE
be	was / were
bring	brought
build	built
buy	bought
can	could
catch	caught
choose	chose
come	came
do	did
draw	drew
drink	drank
drive	drove
eat	ate
fall	fell
feed	fed
find	found
fly	flew
get	got
give	gave
go	went
grow	grew
have (got)	had
hide	hid
hit	hit
hold	held
hurt	hurt
know	knew

INFINITIVE	PAST SIMPLE
learn	learnt / learned
lose	lost
make	made
mean	meant
put	put
read /riːd/	read /red/
ride	rode
run	ran
say	said
see	saw
send	sent
sing	sang
sit	sat
sleep	slept
spell	spelt / spelled
stand	stood
swim	swam
take	took
teach	taught
tell	told
think	thought
throw	threw
understand	understood
wake (up)	woke (up)
wear	wore
write	wrote

Move!
Preparation for the A1 Movers
Cambridge English Qualifications
Student's Book
by Michelle Worgan

Managing Editor: Simona Franzoni
Editors: Linda Pergolini, Lisa Suett
Art Director: Letizia Pigini
Page design: Sergio Elisei
Page layout: Diletta Brutti
Production Manager: Francesco Capitano
Illustrated by: Marta Comito, Giovanni Pierfranceschi, Ivan Zoni

Cover
Cover design: Sergio Elisei
Illustrated by: Marta Comito

© 2021 ELI S.r.l
P.O. Box 6
62019 Recanati
Italy
Tel. +39 071 750701
Fax. +39 071 977851
info@elionline.com
www.elionline.com

Producing educational materials is a complex procedure. While every effort has been made to ensure the correctness of our materials, experience has shown us that inaccuracies are still possible. Every comment or suggestion that we receive will be valuable to us and will allow us to improve our future publications.
Please write to us at: international@elionline.com

Printed by Tecnostampa – Pigini Group Printing Division
Loreto-Trevi, Italy 21.83.288.1

ISBN 978-88-536-3292-0

MONSTER MATHS

Christabell

HOBBIES	Playing games on her laptop computer
SKILL	Technology whizz
FAVOURITE COLOURS	Pink and red
LIVES	Smile Street with Ezzo, Waldo and Whiffy

Ezzo

HOBBIES	Kung fu
STRENGTH	Martial Arts expert
BEST MOVE	Karate kick
FAVOURITE FILMS	Monster action films

Waldo

FAVOURITE FOOD	Dog biscuits
HOBBIES	Biting squeaky toys
STRANGE FACT	Can change shape
OWNER	Ezzo

Whiffy

FAVOURITE FOOD	Cakes with lots of icing
HOBBIES	Playing, dancing
STRANGE FACT	Turns to invisible vapour when afraid and makes a terrible smell

P (a.k.a. Princess)

HOBBIES	Scheming to take over Monster City
STRENGTH	Deadly scream that knocks everybody out
LIKES	Sparkly things, parties

Edgar

HOBBIES	Making machines to take over Monster City
SKILL	Brilliant scientist
BEST INVENTION	Gripping bow tie
BEST FRIEND	P

Flob

HOBBIES	Monster TV
BEST FRIEND	P won't let him have friends, because she doesn't want any
LIKES	Eating yummy food until his tummy is about to pop

Dawn was breaking and most of the monsters in Monster City were asleep. In Smile Street, Ezzo was in bed dreaming that a burglar was trying to get in to the house and was making a lot of noise downstairs.

Suddenly, he opened his eyes and sat up in bed. "I'm not dreaming! That noise is real!" he exclaimed. "Waldo, is that you?" he called. But Waldo didn't appear. Ezzo jumped out of bed. "Something's wrong with Waldo," he thought, trying not to panic.

He ran downstairs and gasped at what he saw. The window was wide open. Even worse, Waldo, Ezzo's loved pet, was missing from his sleeping basket and in his place was a note. "Dear Ezzo, If you want to see Waldo again come to the palace (use the blue door). Don't ring the police or I'll scream. Love from P."

P knows that Ezzo will come to find Waldo, because he's a loyal friend. Put your loyalty sticker in the right place at the front of the book.

① numbers 1 to 1000

In Monster City, monsters always write the numbers of their houses in words. So the postman has to look at words on the envelope and think of them as a number to work out where to deliver the letter!

② Adding 10, 100 and 1000

Ezzo has locked the note in his safe as evidence against P. He has set a difficult code to the safe lock using tens, hundreds and thousands, though.

Adding 10, 100 and 1000 to other numbers to make bigger numbers can sometimes be useful. When adding 10, just add 1 to the tens column. When adding 100, add 1 to the hundreds column. When adding 1000, add 1 to the thousands column.

Th	H	T	U
		2	7
+ 1	0	0	0
1	0	2	7

$$27 + 1000 = 1027$$

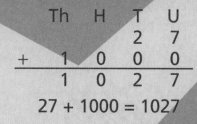

Draw a line from each written number to the numbers on the doors.

1 One hundred and sixty-three

2 Four hundred and fifty-four

3 Four hundred and thirty-nine

4 Seven hundred and six

5 Three hundred and seventy

6 Five hundred and forty-five

7 Seven hundred and sixty-six

8 Three hundred and five

9 Two hundred and twenty

10 One hundred and forty

11 Four hundred and thirty-six

12 Six hundred and sixty-eight

305
454
163
370
545
439
706
436
220
140
766
668

Add up the following sums. Write your answers on the safe doors.

1 6 + 10 =

2 6 + 100 =

3 6 + 1000 =

4 28 + 10 =

5 28 + 100 =

6 28 + 1000 =

7 423 + 10 =

8 423 + 100 =

9 423 + 1000 =

10 207 + 10 =

11 207 + 100 =

12 207 + 1000 =

Ezzo felt anger rising inside him. P and her nasty friends had made trouble before. What were they up to now?

"I've got to rescue Waldo," Ezzo thought to himself. "I'll need help from my friends." He raced to Christabell's room, only to find her already standing in the corridor, looking very worried.

"I found this on Whiffy's door," she said, showing him another note. "I don't usually smell him sleeping next door, but this morning his smell was so strong it seeped through the walls and woke me up," Christabell explained. "I knew he must have been really frightened by something to make a smell that bad, so I rushed in. He's gone and his room is in a mess. It looks as if there's been a struggle."

She read the note out loud, "Dear Christabell, If you want to see Whiffy again, come to the palace (use the red door). Don't ring the police. From Edgar."

3 Subtracting 10, 100 and 1000

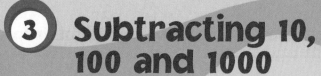

Edgar has taken Whiffy away! Taking away in maths is not as mean! When taking away 10, just subtract 1 from the tens column. When taking away 100, subtract 1 from the hundreds column. When taking away 1000, subtract 1 from the thousands column.

Th	H	T	U
1	6	3	2
−		1	0
1	6	2	2

$$1632 - 10 = 1622$$

4 Totalling money

It's important to be able to total money. That way, you know how much you have and how many things you can buy!

Christabell and Ezzo search their house for money in case P asks for a ransom for Waldo. They find several purses under cushions and beds, and in cupboards and bags. They start to count the money. It's best to start with pounds first, then pence.

Christabell is a very smart girl, I hope Edgar knows what he's taking on! Add the Powers of Deduction sticker to the Smile Street Gang's sheet.

Work out these subtractions and write the answers in the box.

1   4872 – 10 = ⬜

2   4872 – 100 = ⬜

3   4872 – 1000 = ⬜

4   2530 – 10 = ⬜

5   2530 – 100 = ⬜

6   2530 – 1000 = ⬜

7   9284 – 10 = ⬜

8   9284 – 100 = ⬜

9   9284 – 1000 = ⬜

10 3627 – 10 = ⬜

11 4700 – 100 = ⬜

12 3085 – 1000 = ⬜

Write down the total amount of money in each purse.

1    £2 50p

2   £1 20p 10p

3   £1 50p 5p 1p

4   £2 20p 2p 2p

5    £1 50p 10p £2 2p

6    £2 20p 50p 5p

7    £2 £2 20p 10p 2p 2p 50p 5p

8    £2 £1 50p

9    £2 £2 £1 20p 5p

10  £2 £2 20p 20p 1p £2

11  £2 £2 £2 20p £2 2p

12  £1 50p 20p 2p 20p 5p 2p

Ezzo and Christabell swiftly made their way through the city streets. When they reached the palace they found a sign with an arrow painted on it, directing them round to the side of the building. It read, "Go this way."

"I'll go any way I like," Ezzo snapped angrily and reached towards the front door.

"Stop!" Christabell grabbed his hand. "My handbag is fitted with sensors and they're registering electric current running through that door," she explained. "If you touch it, you'll get a terrible electric shock." So they followed the arrow and found two ladders stretching up towards the palace rooftops, leading to two door hatches – one red and one blue. Ezzo climbed up to the blue one and Christabell climbed to the red one, as the notes had asked.

Before they opened the hatchways, they shared a worried look. Who knew what was on the other side?

Christabell is a technology whizz as well as a good friend. Add Electric Sensory Capacity to the list of the goodies' skills.

⑤ Following directions

Ezzo didn't want to follow the sign with an arrow on it, because he was so angry with P. However, sometimes it is useful to be able to follow directions. They help us to get from one place to another.

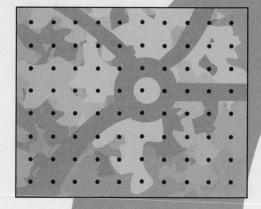

⑥ Converting lengths

The roof of the palace is very high. The hatches are 500 centimetres and 650 centimetres high. But you can make these big numbers smaller by converting them from centimetres to metres.

Remember, a metre is made up of 100 centimetres. You can also write **m** for metre and **cm** for centimetre.

500cm = 5m
650cm = 6.5m

Follow these instructions. Then write the co-ordinates for each place you come to in the boxes.

1 Go to the start sign ⬜ , ⬜

2 Go north 3 spaces. ⬜ , ⬜

3 Turn right and move 4 spaces. ⬜ , ⬜

4 Turn right again and move 2 spaces. ⬜ , ⬜

5 Turn left and move 1 space. ⬜ , ⬜

6 Turn to face north and move 4 spaces. ⬜ , ⬜

7 Make a right angled turn to the left and move 2 spaces. ⬜ , ⬜

8 Go back 1 space. ⬜ , ⬜

9 Turn to face the south and move forward 1 space. ⬜ , ⬜

10 Turn left and move forward 3 spaces. ⬜ , ⬜

11 Turn left and move forward 5 spaces. ⬜ , ⬜

12 Turn to face east and move forward 2 spaces. ⬜ , ⬜

Have you reached the end circle?

Write these centimetre lengths as metre lengths on the rulers.

1 7800cm

2 8500cm

3 9200cm

4 1200cm

5 3200cm

6 7300cm

7 9800cm

8 475cm

9 902cm

10 7890cm

11 9005cm

12 7642cm

The blue hatch opened easily for Ezzo. He found himself standing on a narrow platform high above the floor, in a mouldy-smelling, cobweb-filled attic that stretched the length of the palace.

The only way forward was along a wobbly rope bridge hanging from the roof. Far on the other side of the attic was a large hanging box. Ezzo was shocked to hear Waldo barking from inside it. P had firmly nailed him in, so he couldn't use his special powers to change shape and slip through a crack.

When Christabell opened the red hatch she also found herself on a high platform with an obstacle course in front of her that led to a box. Whiffy's smell was wafting through the sides. He was obviously feeling very scared. The spider webs that festooned the attic looked shiny. "That's weird," Ezzo muttered, touching one nervously. "They're made of thin metal."

P knows Christabell and Ezzo aren't cowards and will rise to the challenge. Add the Bravery skicker to the list.

⑦ Completing patterns

The obstacle course was really tough! The friends went backwards and forwards to find the best way across.

Palindromes are numbers that read the same whether you start from the beginning or the end.

2002 is a palindrome. That means it reads the same even if you start at the end!

⑧ Telling the time

To do something quickly, such as defeating evil monsters, it is important to tell the time on both a digital and an analogue clock.

Digital uses a 24-hour clock. The numbers keep going after 12 noon, so 1pm becomes 13:00 and 2pm becomes 14:00, right up to 24:00, which is 12 midnight.

An analogue clock uses **am** and **pm** to distinguish morning and afternoon, and goes back to 1 when it reaches 12 noon or midnight. So 1pm is in the afternoon and 1am is early in the morning.

analogue

digital

Draw a circle round the numbers in each set that are palindromes. Then make up your own palindrome in the blank boxes.

1 05   123   33

7 890   12321 32

2 4009 121   747

8 67   8434   4004

3 77   345   612

9 2010   3003   3131

4 39   3993   45

10 9865   5555   943

5 6116   546   8888

11 210   3232   3223

6 9009 654 87678

12 987   343   701

Draw a line from the digital time to the matching analogue time. Careful, though - the times are a mixture of am and pm.

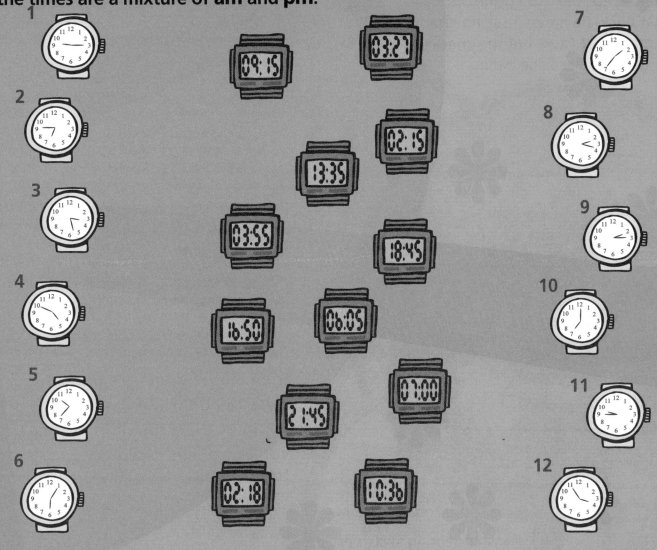

"**I** get the feeling we're being watched," Christabell said, looking across to Ezzo. She glanced up to the roof beams. There they saw small automatic TV cameras pointing down at them. The cameras swivelled to follow their every move.

"Someone's gone to a lot of trouble to set this up," Ezzo murmured. "I guess they're expecting a good show," Christabell nodded. She waved at the cameras cheekily.

Christabell was right. In a hidden room, P, Edgar and Flob were sitting in front of a large TV screen, waiting to be entertained. The obstacle courses had been set up, because of an argument between P and Edgar. It was still going on.

"Ezzo will win easily over Christabell," P declared. "He's too dumb," Edgar spat back. He hated P saying nice things about Ezzo, but the angrier he got, the more she did it.

The goodies' dealings with P and Edgar in the past have made their Bad Monster Sensing Skills very keen. Add this to the list.

9 Multiplying by 10, 100 and 1000

Christabell is very good at multiplication! So she could easily work out how many cameras were watching her and Ezzo.

If you multiply a number by 10, you move all the digits in the number 1 place to the left and fill the space with a zero.

If you multiply a number by 100, you move all the digits in the number 2 places to the left and fill the space with 2 zeros.

If you multiply a number by 1000, you move all the digits in the number 3 places to the left and fill the space with 3 zeros.

$$63 \times 10 = 630$$
$$63 \times 100 = 6300$$
$$63 \times 1000 = 63000$$

10 Dividing by 10, 100 and 1000

Dividing is the inverse of multiplication. Inverse means the opposite!

If you divide a number by 10, you move all the digits 1 place to the right.

If you divide a number by 100, then all the digits are moved 2 places to the right.

If you divide a number by 1000, you move all the digits 3 places to the right.

$$6000 \div 10 = 600$$
$$6000 \div 100 = 60$$
$$6000 \div 1000 = 6$$

Do these multiplication sums and write the numbers in the boxes.

1   45 × 10 =

2   98 × 100 =

3   40 × 100 =

4   65 × 1000 =

5   203 × 100 =

6   8 × 1000 =

7   863 × 100 =

8   900 × 1000 =

9   73 × 100 =

10 230 × 10 =

11 67 × 100 =

12 414 × 1000 =

Write down the answers to these division sums in the boxes.

1   40 ÷ 10 =

2   500 ÷ 10 =

3   600 ÷ 100 =

4   870 ÷ 10 =

5   7000 ÷ 100 =

6   9800 ÷ 100 =

7   780000 ÷ 1000 =

8   572000 ÷ 1000 =

9   30000 ÷ 100 =

10 760 ÷ 10 =

11 7600 ÷ 100 =

12 940000 ÷ 1000 =

"**C**hristabell is smarter. She's a winner," Edgar insisted, knowing that praising Christabell annoyed P. As they carried on arguing, Flob settled down to watch.

"I love TV game shows!" he cried. "Tell me the rules. Is the winner the first one to reach their box and rescue their friend? What's the prize?" he asked. The others ignored him and carried on bickering.

"Christabell is a weakling." "Ezzo is rubbish."

"I've rigged up a few surprises for your stupid hero," Edgar yelled at P. "I've done the same for your swotty girl," P snapped. "Then let the show begin!" Flob cried and he pressed a button. Ezzo's platform fell away and he had to leap onto the rope bridge. The same happened to Christabell. "Are you alright?" Ezzo called over to her.

"Don't bother about her. Hurry up and win!" P shouted at the TV screens.

P has a soft spot for Ezzo, because of his amazing physical strength and kung fu skills. Put the sticker on the sheet.

11 Weights

We can measure weight in kilogrammes, which we sometimes write as kg. So 34 kilogrammes could be shortened to 34kg.

The rope that Ezzo has to cross can hold 50kg. Ezzo isn't that heavy. But if he was, the rope would break.

12 Working out the time

Flob loves TV game shows. But to watch them, he needs to be able to work out what time they're on.

When working out the time, it is easiest to add on the hours and then the minutes. Remember, there are 24 hours in a day and 60 minutes in an hour.

Write down the combined weights of the monsters as they try to cross the bridge together. Put a tick if they are under the 50kg limit and a cross if they are over.

16kg   30kg   11kg 20kg 22kg   26kg 13kg

1   Christabell and P = ☐ ☐

2   Edgar and Waldo = ☐ ☐

3   Flob and Edgar = ☐ ☐

4   Ezzo and Whiffy = ☐ ☐

5   P and Ezzo = ☐ ☐

6   Waldo and Whiffy = ☐ ☐

7   Christabell and Whiffy = ☐ ☐

8   Christabell, Ezzo and Whiffy = ☐ ☐

9   Flob, P and Edgar = ☐ ☐

10 Waldo, Flob and P = ☐ ☐

11 P, Flob and Christabell = ☐ ☐

12 Ezzo, Whiffy and P = ☐ ☐

Use the information on this TV programme guide to work out the time each game show ends. Write your answers in the empty column.

	Show times Starting time	Length of show		Finishing time
1	9:30am	2 hours		_____
2	10:45pm	50 min		_____
3	12:15pm	45 min		_____
4	12:45pm	1hr 30min		_____
5	2:50pm	40 min		_____
6	3:30pm	20 min		_____
7	9:30am	1 hour 20 min		_____
8	10:45pm	30 min		_____
9	12:15pm	I hour 20 min		_____
10	12:45pm	2 hours 10 min		_____
11	2:50pm	2 hours		_____
12	3:30pm	50 min		_____

At first, Ezzo went faster than Christabell across the obstacle course.

"I think I'll wake up my friend who made all those cobwebs," Edgar muttered menacingly. He pressed a button and a giant robot spider dropped from the ceiling onto Ezzo. "Fight that! You lose!" Edgar cackled. Ezzo struggled to fight a creature with so many legs, all grabbing him at once. He sank to his knees under the weight.

"We'll see about that," P snapped and she pressed a button, tipping a barrel of sticky green goo over Christabell. "Now she doesn't look so pretty!" P laughed and made one of the TV cameras zoom in on Christabell's goo-covered face. Christabell slipped and slid around on the goo, but she didn't fall. Instead, she started to throw handfuls of it over towards the robot spider on Ezzo's platform.

"Stop that! Get on with winning!" Edgar screamed.

One thing the baddies didn't bank on is the Smile Street Gang's problem solving powers. Pop the sticker on the picture.

(13) Lines of symmetry

Look at this cobweb, designed by Edgar. It has 3 lines of symmetry. A line of symmetry is the line where you fold a shape so that each side fits exactly onto the other.

(14) Fractions of shapes

Edgar wants to work out how to make more cobwebs fast! He could do that by breaking his cobwebs into smaller pieces, using fractions.

In a fraction, the bottom number tells you how many parts something has been divided into, and the top number tells you how many of those bits we have.

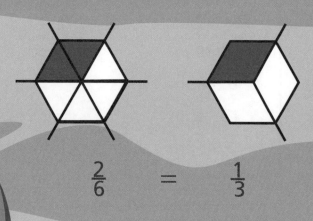

$$\frac{2}{6} = \frac{1}{3}$$

Look at each of these shapes and draw the lines of symmetry. Some shapes will have more than 1 line of symmetry.

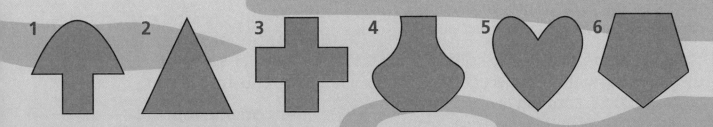

1   2   3   4   5   6

Look at these unfinished shapes. Finish drawing them to make sure they are symmetrical.

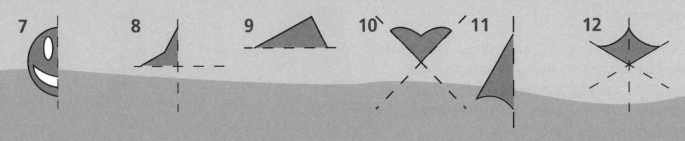

7   8   9   10   11   12

Look at these cobwebs, which have been divided into smaller pieces. Write down the fraction of the pink area for each one.

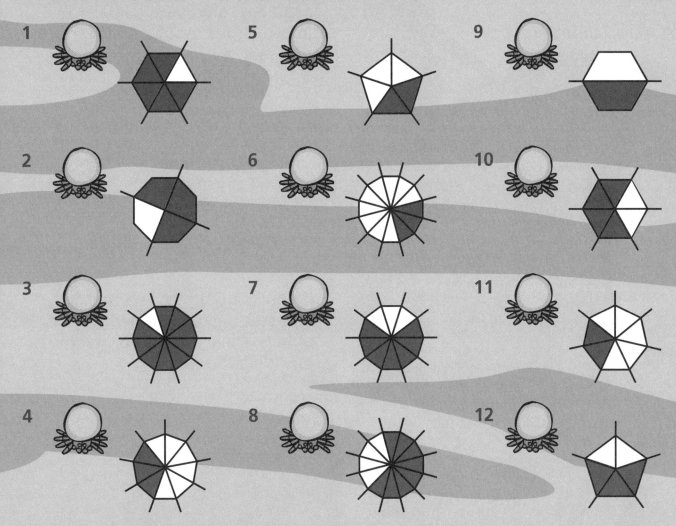

1   5   9

2   6   10

3   7   11

4   8   12

C hristabell was good at throwing and she soon plastered the spider in goo. Once its controls got gooey it stopped working.

"Thanks," Ezzo called over to her and they both began the next part of the obstacle course. Ezzo had to walk across a thin plank like a tightrope, as Edgar sent flying robot creatures to buzz around his head. He managed to get across, but Christabell really struggled on her plank. Her boots were covered in goo, so she slipped and almost fell off.

"Hold on, Christabell," Ezzo cried. He grabbed one of the biggest flying robots, hung on tightly to its feet and leapt off his plank. The watching monsters gasped as Ezzo pointed the flying robot towards Christabell. "This robot can't carry us both," he cried. "Here, Christabell. You have it. Hold on tight and fly to the boxes!"

"No!" P shouted angrily.

Edgar may be good at making robots, but Ezzo is good at using them to his advantage. Add Robot Model No. 3 to the goodies' sheet.

15 Addition short cuts

Ezzo wants to find a short cut across the plank, so he tries to remember some of the maths short cuts he's learnt.

Here's one he remembered: if you are adding on 99, add on 100 and take away 1. So if your sum is 23 + 99, make it:

$$23 + 100 = 123 - 1 = 122$$

If you are adding on 98, add on 100 and take away 2.

16 Problem solving

Edgar numbers all his robots so he knows which are the latest versions. Edgar is a fantastic problem solver and constantly improves his robots, which makes him such a dangerous enemy!

If you're going to be a bad monster buster, you need to be able to solve number problems as quickly as Edgar.

Use short cuts to do each sum and write your answer in the box.

1 63 + 99 =

2 48 + 98 =

3 37 + 97 =

4 90 + 99 =

5 132 + 98 =

6 165 + 99 =

7 69 + 96 =

8 137 + 97 =

9 129 + 98 =

10 215 + 99 =

11 58 + 96 =

12 106 + 97 =

Work out the answers to these questions. Then draw a line to the correct robot.

1 Who is 132 + 43? _____

2 Who is 7 × 9? _____

3 Who is 49 ÷ 7? _____

4 Who is 97 − 26? _____

5 Who is 8 × 7? _____

6 Who is 81 ÷ 9? _____

7 Who is 47 + 10? _____

8 Who is 47 × 100? _____

9 Who is 900 ÷ 10? _____

10 Who is 200 − 99? _____

11 Who is 45 + 98? _____

12 Who is 4 × 4? _____

"He's going to lose," Edgar grinned. "Christabell is a cheat!" P snapped back. "Shut up both of you. Watch the show," Flob told them.

Ezzo balanced on her plank and passed the flying robot to Christabell. He climbed along her obstacle course, easily crossing the plank, then swung on a rope across a gap towards the boxes. Meanwhile Christabell flew along next to him, making sure he was alright.

"What a good team!" Flob cried excitedly. "They're not a team. Come on Christabell!" Edgar shouted. "Come on Ezzo!" P called out. "They're going to finish together," Flob grinned. Sure enough, Ezzo and Christabell reached the boxes at exactly the same time and no matter how often Edgar re-ran the picture as an action replay, the result looked the same. "Teamwork. That's their secret," Flob decided. "Shut up!" P and Edgar shouted, angry that their nasty competition had been ruined.

Flob knows that Ezzo and Christabell make a good team. Put the handy rope that Ezzo swings across on the goodies' list.

17 Area

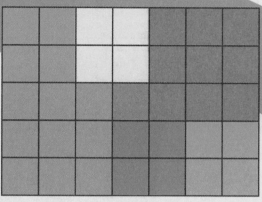

7cm

5cm

We can find out the area of a surface by multiplying its length by its width.

A surface that is 7cm long and 5cm wide equals an area of 35 square centimetres. We write this as 35cm²

$$7cm \times 5cm = 35cm^2$$

18 number teams

While Christabell was working as part of a team, it struck her that numbers work as a team too. Numbers work in teams of 3. For example, if you take three numbers such as

3   5   15

they work in variety of ways.

$$3 \times 5 = 15$$
$$5 \times 3 = 15$$

$$15 \div 3 = 5$$
$$15 \div 5 = 3$$

**Count the number of squares along the sides to find the width and length.
Then write down the area of each surface in cm².**

1 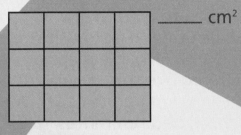 _____ cm²

6 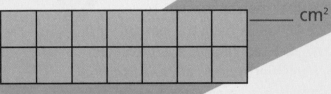 _____ cm²

2 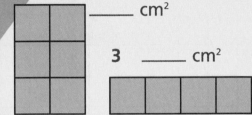 _____ cm²

3 _____ cm²

7 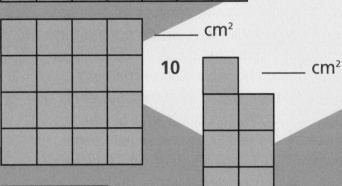 _____ cm²

10 _____ cm²

4 _____ cm²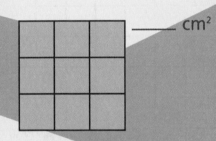

8 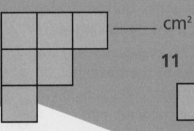 _____ cm²

11 _____ cm²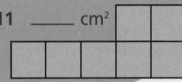

5 _____ cm²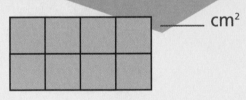

9 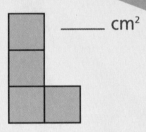 _____ cm²

12 _____ cm²

**Fill these boxes with the missing times table answers - both multiplication
and division facts!**

1   $3 \times 4 =$

   $12 \div 4 =$

5   $12 \times 5 =$

   $60 \div 5 =$

9   $12 \times 3 =$

   $36 \div 3 =$

2   $8 \times 5 =$

   $40 \div 5 =$

6   $9 \times 3 =$

   $27 \div 3 =$

10 $10 \times 10 =$

   $100 \div 10 =$

3   $6 \times 3 =$

   $18 \div 3 =$

7   $8 \times 2 =$

   $16 \div 2 =$

11 $7 \times 5 =$

   $35 \div 5 =$

4   $11 \times 2 =$

   $22 \div 2 =$

8   $4 \times 4 =$

   $16 \div 4 =$

12 $12 \times 4 =$

   $48 \div 4 =$

Christabell opened the first box using her handbag-sized, super-power magnet to remove the nails from the box. At first she couldn't see Whiffy, but she could smell him! Whiffy had got really scared and turned into smelly vapour! As soon as he saw his friends, he reappeared and gave Christabell a big, smelly hug. Next, Ezzo did a sharp karate chop to a side of the box, shattering the nails. Waldo leapt out of his box into Ezzo's arms. "Stupid goody-goody monsters! You've ruined the show!" Edgar growled. "Let's capture them all," P hissed nastily. Edgar pressed another button. A giant hammer dropped down from the ceiling and smashed up the obstacle courses, leaving the four friends sitting on top of the boxes, swinging from the attic roof. "Let's see you escape from that," Edgar sneered. "Oh good. The show hasn't finished yet," Flob grinned happily and settled down to watch again.

(19) Handling grids

As the friends make their escape, they need to plan their way back to Smile Street. Look at the map of the area. When a map is numbered like this, it helps us to find something quite easily. We call these grid references.

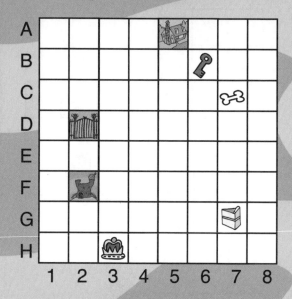

(20) Giving change

When the friendly monsters are free from the palace, they plan to go shopping. When you give shopkeepers money, you will usually receive coins as change, especially if you use a £5 or £10 note.

If Ezzo had £10 to spend, and he bought a DVD about kung fu costing £3.75, he would have £6.25 change.

Christabell had another clever gadget in her handbag - her super-power magnet. Pop it on the sheet.

Using the map opposite, write down the answers to questions 1 to 7. Then complete the map by following the instructions in 8 to 15.

1 What would Christabell find in grid reference 3H? _____

2 What would Waldo like to eat in grid reference 7C? _____

3 What would Flob find in 7G? _____

4 What would the friends find in 2F? _____

5 What is in the wall at 2D? _____

6 Which grid reference has the key to unlock the gate? _____

7 Which grid reference is the friend's house in Smile Street? _____

8 Draw a tree in 6D.

9 Draw a bridge in 7B.

10 Draw a river running under the bridge.
   The river runs from 6A to 8D.

11 Draw Edgar's glasses in 5G.

12 Draw Whiffy's smelly vapour in 8H.

Write down the change Ezzo would have from £10 if he bought these things.

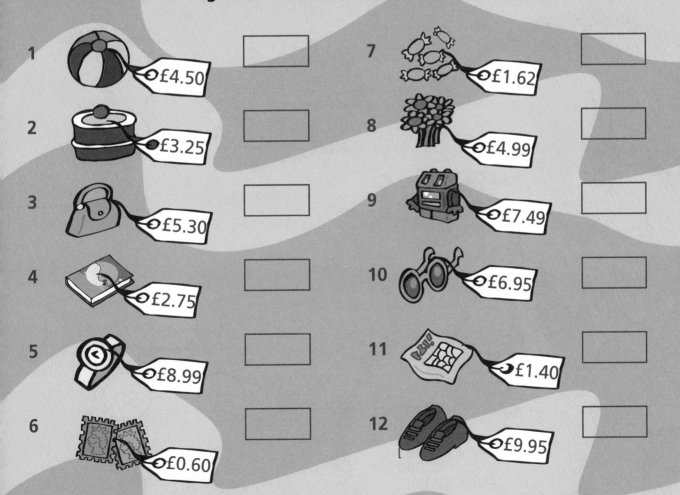

1 £4.50 [ ]

2 £3.25 [ ]

3 £5.30 [ ]

4 £2.75 [ ]

5 £8.99 [ ]

6 £0.60 [ ]

7 £1.62 [ ]

8 £4.99 [ ]

9 £7.49 [ ]

10 £6.95 [ ]

11 £1.40 [ ]

12 £9.95 [ ]

Edgar switched on a microphone to speak to the stranded monsters. "We will only rescue you if you promise to leave Monster City forever," he announced. P pushed him aside and spoke into the microphone herself.

"Except for you, Ezzo. I'll rescue you now," she called. "Leave the others behind. They're just weaklings, but you're a hero. You don't need them, Ezzo. You can be in my gang," she begged him.

"I'll never abandon my friends!" Ezzo shouted out. "We don't need you to rescue us. We'll do it ourselves," he added defiantly.

"Ooh, I love this show!" Flob clapped delightedly. "I think it's boring. The stars are so nice to each other it makes me sick," Edgar scowled. P sighed. "Ezzo is very brave, but he's so annoying sometimes," she remarked. "Why can't he be just a little teensy bit more rotten?"

You don't need to be rotten when you have a karate kick like Ezzo's. Add the karate sticker to the picture.

21 Amazing number 9

Being in P's gang would not be nice. Find out which numbers are in 9's gang. All numbers that can be divided evenly by 9 can also be added together to make 9.

$$72 \div 9 = 8$$

Add the digits of 72: $7 + 2 = 9$

You can find out if really big numbers can be divided by 9 equally too in just the same way.

$$288 \div 9$$

Add the digits of 288: $2 + 8 + 8 = 18$. Now add $1 + 8 = 9$.

22 number triangles

Just like the monsters are in groups, each triangle can make a group of 4 sums, 2 multiplying and 2 dividing.

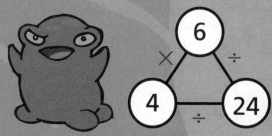

This triangle shows:

$$4 \times 6 = 24 \quad 6 \times 4 = 24$$
$$24 \div 6 = 4 \quad 24 \div 4 = 6$$

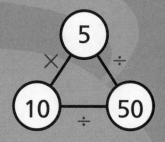

$$5 \times 10 = 50 \quad 10 \times 5 = 50$$
$$50 \div 10 = 5 \quad 50 \div 5 = 10$$

Can these numbers be divided by 9? Write Yes or No beside each one.

1 162 _____
2 144 _____
3 45 _____
4 886 _____

5 206 _____
6 225 _____
7 810 _____
8 2406 _____

9 648 _____
10 1296 _____
11 63 _____
12 90 _____

Write down the 4 sums and answers for each of these triangles.

1 8 × ÷ 3 ÷ 24 _____ _____

2 4 × ÷ 5 ÷ 20 _____ _____

3 7 × ÷ 6 ÷ 42 _____ _____

4 5 × ÷ 8 ÷ 40 _____ _____

5 2 × ÷ 9 ÷ 18 _____ _____

6 4 × ÷ 3 ÷ 12 _____ _____

7 6 × ÷ 4 ÷ 24 _____ _____

8 9 × ÷ 4 ÷ 36 _____ _____

9 10 × ÷ 3 ÷ 30 _____ _____

10 8 × ÷ 6 ÷ 48 _____ _____

11 6 × ÷ 10 ÷ 60 _____ _____

12 2 × ÷ 4 ÷ 8 _____ _____

Ezzo whispered in Waldo's ear, asking him to use his special powers to make himself round and flat. Then he beckoned the others.

"Ready, team?"

"Ready," Christabell and Whiffy replied.

Ezzo held on to Whiffy's legs. Whiffy held on to Christabell, who held on to Waldo. "One, two, three. Jump!" Ezzo cried, and they leapt into space.

"Wow!" Flob gasped. "How cool is that?" The TV screens showed the Smile Street friends floating softly down towards the ground underneath a parachute-shaped Waldo.

"Don't let them escape!" P shouted.

Edgar activated his clever bow tie. It shot out like a long arm and, at double speed, it began pressing all the buttons in the room, trying to activate every robot monster he had.

23 Block graphs

Activating all the robots isn't as easy as it sounds. There were loads of buttons in different colours for Edgar's bow tie to press. So he decided to use a block graph. These are useful to count objects very quickly.

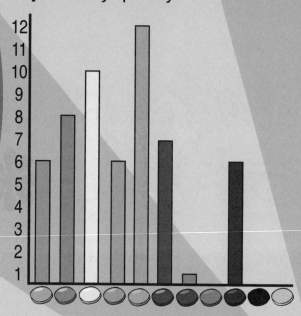

24 Fractions and percentages

Look at this monster square. It contains 100 squares, all different colours. We can find out things about these colours using fractions and percentages. 50 of the 100 squares are yellow. $\frac{50}{100}$ is 50% or $\frac{1}{2}$. 25 of the 100 squares are lilac. $\frac{25}{100}$ is 25% or $\frac{1}{4}$.

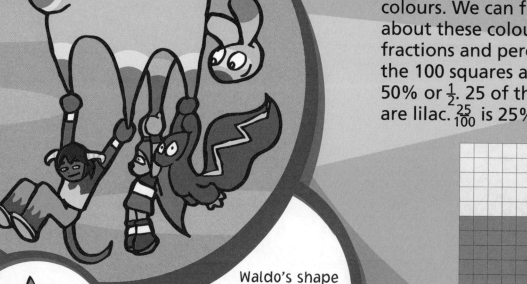

Waldo's shape - changing powers have come in handy just at the right time. Put Waldo's skill on the sheet.

Below are some questions and some instructions. Use the block graph to help you complete each one.

1 Which colour is there the most of? _____

2 How many more red buttons are there than lilac? ☐

3 Which is the most frequently occurring number? _____

4 More robots appeared with 5 silver buttons. Add them to the graph

5 There are half the amount of silver buttons than of another colour. Which colour is that? _____

6 What can you tell about the brown buttons? _____

7 How many colours are there with fewer buttons than pink? ☐

8 How many buttons are there altogether? ☐

9 Add a column for black buttons. The number of black buttons is greater than the number of pink and less than the number of yellow.

10 If 3 orange buttons stop working, how many working orange buttons are left? ☐

11 Write the colours in order, starting with the colour with the most buttons, down to the colour which has the fewest buttons.

_____ _____ _____

_____ _____ _____

_____ _____ _____

_____ _____

12 There are 10 robots. If each robot has the same number of buttons, how many buttons does each robot have? ☐

Use the monster square to answer these questions.

1 There are 10 red squares. What is the fraction?

2 There are 4 green squares. What is the fraction?

3 25 squares are lilac. What is the percentage?

4 50 are yellow. What is the percentage?

5 2 are white. What is the fraction?

6 5 are blue. What is the fraction?

7 There are 3 orange squares. What is the fraction?

8 There is 1 pink square. What is the percentage?

9 What colour are $\frac{1}{2}$ of the squares? _____

10 What colour are $\frac{1}{4}$ of the squares? _____

11 What percentage do all the squares that aren't yellow added together make?

_____, _____,

_____, _____,

_____, _____,

_____, _____

12 Which colour could also be written as 10%? _____

The Smile Street team reached the attic floor, then ran towards the nearest door. They made their way downstairs, but had to trip, push, punch and dodge all kinds of robots sent by Edgar. Ezzo gave a mighty kung fu kick to a robot dinosaur and at the same time dodged a giant robot fly. Christabell bashed a robot snake over the head with her bag, then spun round and stamped on the toes of a robot gorilla.

They reached the locked and electrified front door of the palace. Ranks of robots gathered behind them, growling, hissing and roaring. Whiffy was terrified and his overpowering smell was making the others feel giddy. A robot crocodile tried to snap at Ezzo's heels, missed and not only crunched through a wire, electrocuting itself, but also cut off the electricity current to the door. "Ready, steady, go!" Ezzo ordered. The friends all ran at the locked door together, Ezzo leaping through the air with all the power he had.

Ezzo's power leap has never been so useful! Pop the sticker on the goodies' skill list.

(25) Subtraction short cuts

The friends wish they had been able to find a short cut to escape. There are many short cuts in maths. Here is one for subtraction.

If you have 2 big numbers like 97 – 64, do the sum like this.

Round down 64 to 60.

$$97 - 60 = 37$$

Now take away the remaining 4.

$$37 - 4 = 33$$

(26) Dividing fractions

By the time the friendly monsters had finished fighting the robots, there was a fraction of the robots left.

Remember, $\frac{1}{10}$ of 60 is the same as $60 \div 10$.

So $\frac{6}{10}$ of 60 would be

$$60 \div 10 \times 6 = 36$$

Write down the answers to these questions using the subtraction short cut to help you.

1 58 − 43 =

5 86 − 32 =

9 108 − 72 =

2 89 − 65 =

6 47 − 26 =

10 326 − 135 =

3 36 − 17 =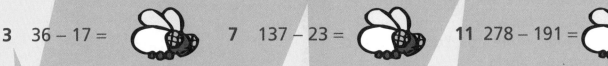

7 137 − 23 =

11 278 − 191 =

4 75 − 23 =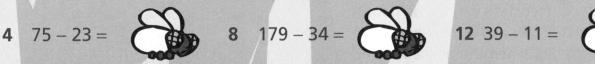

8 179 − 34 =

12 39 − 11 =

Write down the answers to these fraction divisions.

1 $\frac{1}{10}$ of 50 =

7 $\frac{3}{7}$ of 56 =

2 $\frac{3}{10}$ of 60 =

8 $\frac{6}{10}$ of 80 =

3 $\frac{1}{8}$ of 64 =

9 $\frac{7}{9}$ of 72 =

4 $\frac{7}{8}$ of 64 =

10 $\frac{5}{7}$ of 35 =

5 $\frac{3}{5}$ of 45 =

11 $\frac{2}{6}$ of 30 =

6 $\frac{12}{20}$ of 40 =

12 $\frac{1}{4}$ of 16 =

The door burst open and the Smile Street friends tumbled out. Ezzo slammed the front door in the faces of the chasing robots. Christabell kicked off her boots and jammed them under the door to keep it shut while the robots began hammering against the inside. "Run!" Ezzo shouted.

P, Edgar and Flob were left staring at blank TV screens. "Is the show over?" Flob asked. "It was really fun." "Shut up," Edgar growled, furious to have lost again.

The Smile Street monsters ran to the police station in Monster City and explained about the kidnapping. But when the police arrived at the palace, Edgar and P pretended to know nothing. "Those Smile Street monsters are terrible liars. Christabell is the worst!" P told them.

"Ezzo is the worst," disagreed Edgar, and the two of them began to argue all over again.

Christabel's super fibre boots are strong as well as stylish. P should take a leaf out of her fashion book. Add the boots sticker.

(27) Rotational symmetry

As the friends tumbled out of the door, they rolled over and over. Shapes can also rotate to fit back into the same space. Some shapes can fit into their own space more than once when rotated.

(28) Number patterns

Number patterns are a special arrangement of numbers or shapes, where they repeat or change in a regular way, just like P constantly repeats her mean behaviour!

2 4 6 8, who does P appreciate... Herself!

Tick the shapes that can rotate and fit back into their own space more than once.

1 ☐

5 ☐

9 ☐

2 ☐

6 ☐

10 ☐

3 ☐

7 ☐

11 ☐

4 ☐

8 ☐

12 ☐

Finish these number patterns by writing the next numbers in the boxes.

1 2   4   8   16   ☐ ☐

7 70   63   56   49   ☐ ☐

2 160 80   40   20   ☐ ☐

8 1   3   5   7   ☐ ☐

3 20   30   40   50   ☐ ☐

9 25   30   35   40   ☐ ☐

4 81   72   63   54   ☐ ☐

10 634 636 638 640   ☐ ☐

5 6   3   9   4   13 ☐ ☐

11 90   80   70   60   ☐ ☐

6 75   70   65   60   ☐ ☐

12 20   24   28   32   ☐ ☐

Flob ignored their arguing and began to chat to the police. "I saw this amazing TV show this morning. Did you watch it?" he asked them. "Ezzo and Christabell were very good. They rescued their friends and then escaped by parachute!" he explained.

"Shut up!" Edgar kicked him, but it was too late. The police arrested the three evil monsters for kidnapping and took them to jail, gagging P to stop her screaming.

"I hate the way the Smile Street monsters always insist on helping each other out," Edgar spat as the police locked their jail cell. "Maybe we should do the same. We could work as a team and help each other. Then we might escape," Flob suggested hopefully.

"Don't be dumb. That's a stupid idea, Flob. We're bad," P and Edgar both turned on him. Flob shrugged his shoulders. "It was just an idea I saw on TV," he muttered.

29 Properties of shapes

The parachute on the TV show was made of beautiful shapes sewn together. Shapes have properties – that means how many edges and corners they have.

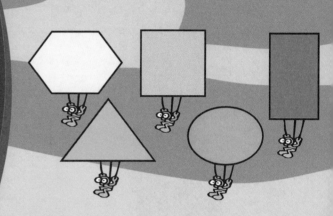

30 Problem solving

What a problem the monster friends have had. But they used all their powers and their brains, and they managed to solve it in the end.

Now see what you have also learnt from their adventure.

If the baddies had teamwork skills like the Smile Street Gang, they'd save themselves a lot of bother. Put the final sticker on the list.

Complete the table by adding the number of edges, corners and faces.

		Number of edges	Number of corners	Number of faces (3D shapes only)
1	square	_____	_____	_____
2	circle	_____	_____	_____
3	hexagon	_____	_____	_____
4	rectangle	_____	_____	_____
5	pentagon	_____	_____	_____
6	octagon	_____	_____	_____
7	triangle	_____	_____	_____
8	decagon	_____	_____	_____
9	cube	_____	_____	_____
10	sphere	_____	_____	_____
11	triangular prism	_____	_____	_____
12	cylinder	_____	_____	_____

Write the answers to these problems in the spaces.

1 Edgar bought his bow tie 2 years ago for £4.50. It has doubled its original price each year. How much is it worth? _____

2 The jail cell is 2.5m wide. How many jail cells can fit side by side along a 10m wall? _____

3 If Flob watches each programme on his TV for 15 minutes, how many programmes can he watch in 2 hours? _____

4 If the parachute has 16 sections on it and 4 of them are red, what fraction of the parachute is red? _____

5 There are 97 steps in the palace. Only 82 of them are safe. How many are dangerous? _____

6 One side of the front of a symmetrical house has 16 entire windows. How many windows does the entire front have? _____

7 6 monsters find 3 boxes of sweets. Each box has 10 sweets in it. How many sweets would each monster get? _____

8 A snake robot has 32 spots on it. $\frac{1}{4}$ of the spots are flashing. How many of the spots are flashing? _____

9 Christabell finds £10 in her pocket. She buys a treat for each of her friends and they come to £7.99. How much change does she get? _____

10 A robot falls over and the batteries fall out. 2 batteries roll under a chair, Flob picks up 3 and 7 fall under the floorboards. How many batteries does the robot need? _____

11 The number of the goodies house is odd. It is bigger than 234 but smaller than 239 and can be divided by 5. What is the number? _____

12 A box has 16 packets of socks in it. There are 8 pairs of socks in each packet. How many pairs of monster socks are there? _____

Answers

Test 1 Numbers 1 to 1000
1	163	5	370	9	220
2	454	6	545	10	140
3	439	7	766	11	436
4	706	8	305	12	668

Test 2 Adding 10, 100 and 1000
1. $6 + 10 = 16$
2. $6 + 100 = 106$
3. $6 + 1000 = 1006$
4. $28 + 10 = 38$
5. $28 + 100 = 128$
6. $28 + 1000 = 1028$
7. $423 + 10 = 433$
8. $423 + 100 = 523$
9. $423 + 1000 = 1423$
10. $207 + 10 = 217$
11. $207 + 100 = 307$
12. $207 + 1000 = 1207$

Test 3 Subtracting 10, 100 and 1000
1. $4872 - 10 = 4862$
2. $4872 - 100 = 4772$
3. $4872 - 1000 = 3872$
4. $2530 - 10 = 2520$
5. $2530 - 100 = 2430$
6. $2530 - 1000 = 1530$
7. $9284 - 10 = 9274$
8. $9284 - 100 = 9184$
9. $9284 - 1000 = 8284$
10. $3627 - 10 = 3617$
11. $4700 - 100 = 4600$
12. $3085 - 1000 = 2085$

Test 4 Totalling money
1	£2.50	7	£4.89
2	£1.30	8	£3.50
3	£1.56	9	£5.25
4	£2.24	10	£6.41
5	£1.64	11	£8.22
6	£2.75	12	£1.99

Test 5 Following directions
1	1A	7	4F
2	1D	8	5F
3	5D	9	5E
4	5B	10	8E
5	6B	11	8J
6	6F	12	10J

Test 6 Converting lengths
1. 78m
2. 85m
3. 92m
4. 12m
5. 32m
6. 73m
7. 98m
8. 4.75m
9. 9.02m
10. 78.90m
11. 90.05m
12. 76.42m

Test 7 Completing patterns
1. 33
2. 121, 747
3. 77
4. 3993
5. 6116, 8888
6. 9009, 87678
7. 12321
8. 4004
9. 3003
10. 5555
11. 3223
12. 343

Test 8 Telling the time
1	09:15	7	13:35
2	18:45	8	02:18
3	03:27	9	02:15
4	16:50	10	07:00
5	10:36	11	21:45
6	06:05	12	03:55

Test 9 Multiplying by 10, 100 and 1000
1. $45 \times 10 = 450$
2. $98 \times 100 = 9800$
3. $40 \times 100 = 4000$
4. $65 \times 1000 = 65000$
5. $203 \times 100 = 20300$
6. $8 \times 1000 = 8000$
7. $863 \times 100 = 86300$
8. $900 \times 1000 = 900000$
9. $73 \times 100 = 7300$
10. $230 \times 10 = 2300$
11. $67 \times 100 = 6700$
12. $414 \times 1000 = 414000$

Test 10 Dividing by 10, 100 and 1000
1. $40 \div 10 = 4$
2. $500 \div 10 = 50$
3. $600 \div 100 = 6$
4. $870 \div 10 = 87$
5. $7000 \div 100 = 70$
6. $9800 \div 100 = 98$
7. $780000 \div 1000 = 780$
8. $572000 \div 1000 = 572$
9. $30000 \div 100 = 300$
10. $760 \div 10 = 76$
11. $7600 \div 100 = 76$
12. $94000 \div 1000 = 940$

Test 11 Weight
1	36kg ✔	5	42kg ✔	9	76kg ✗
2	37kg ✔	6	24kg ✔	10	61kg ✗
3	56kg ✗	7	29kg ✔	11	66kg ✗
4	35kg ✔	8	51kg ✗	12	55kg ✗

Test 12 Working out the time
1	11:30am	7	10:50am
2	11:35pm	8	11:15pm
3	1:00pm	9	1:35pm
4	2:15pm	10	2:55pm
5	3:30pm	11	4:50pm
6	3:50pm	12	4:20pm

Test 13 Lines of symmetry

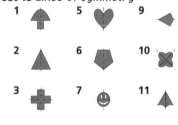

Test 14 Fractions of shapes
1	$\frac{5}{6}$	5	$\frac{2}{5}$	9	$\frac{1}{2}$
2	$\frac{3}{4}$	6	$\frac{3}{12}$ or $\frac{1}{4}$	10	$\frac{4}{6}$ or $\frac{2}{3}$
3	$\frac{9}{10}$	7	$\frac{3}{10}$	11	$\frac{2}{7}$
4	$\frac{3}{9}$ or $\frac{1}{3}$	8	$\frac{8}{12}$ or $\frac{2}{3}$	12	$\frac{3}{5}$

Test 15 Addition short cuts
1	$63 + 99 = 162$	7	$69 + 96 = 165$
2	$48 + 98 = 146$	8	$137 + 97 = 234$
3	$37 + 97 = 134$	9	$129 + 98 = 227$
4	$90 + 99 = 189$	10	$215 + 99 = 314$
5	$132 + 98 = 230$	11	$58 + 96 = 154$
6	$165 + 99 = 264$	12	$106 + 97 = 203$

Test 16 Problem solving 1
1	175	7	57
2	63	8	4700
3	7	9	90
4	71	10	101
5	56	11	143
6	9	12	16